The Gates of Hell:
All Roads Lead to Rome

ISBN 0-9708598-8-0

The Gates of Hell

All Roads Lead to Rome

by

Kathleen Keating

Visit Our Website!
www.countingcouppress.com

Published by Counting Coup Press, Inc.
PO Box 352
Ainsworth, NE 69210

This edition published 2001
by Counting Coup Press, Inc.
ISBN 0-9708598-9-9

Printed in the United States of America

For The Immaculate Heart

Table of Contents

Chapter One

One of the most important breakthroughs in science could be the cracking of the Bible Code. The existence of the code has been speculated upon for centuries. So, when the discovery was made, rabbis, scientists and researchers rejoiced.

To understand the code and its nature, it is necessary to look at the history of the Bible, particularly; the first five books of the Bible, called the Torah. The Torah is sacred not only to Jews, but to Christians and to Muslims as well.

According to Jewish tradition, God dictated the first five books of the Bible to Moses, letter by letter. This is the key to understanding the Code. As this tradition was passed down through thousands of years, there was also an accompanying tradition, which stated that in those dictated letters to Moses, God had encrypted messages for us. That is why the books were dictated so precisely, and the rabbis, who duplicated the Torah, took extreme care.

In the 18th Century, a brilliant Lithuanian rabbi, Elijah Solomon, made quite a statement: "All that was, is, and will be unto the end of time is included in the Torah."

Rabbi Solomon had managed to memorize every single word of the Torah, estimated to be in the millions of words. Further, Soloman was a noted mathematician with a flawless reputation. People took what he had to say to heart. Solomon was not one to speak metaphorically. He was literally saying, "…and not merely in a general sense, but including the details of every person individually, and the most minute details of everything that happened to him from the day of his birth until his death, likewise of every kind of animal and beast and living thing that exists, and of herbage, and of all that grows or is inert."

That was a profound statement and it certainly has been tested repeatedly. Each challenge has been met with astounding results.

For example, Rabbi Moses ben Nachman, or Ramban as he was known, was an incredible genius. He was teaching about the Song of Moses, which can be found in Deuteronomy 32, when he suddenly declared that all of Israel's history could be found in these passages. Ramban had an equally gifted student who was appalled at the rabbi's assertions. The student told Ramban that unless he could prove what he was saying, that he would never listen to another word from him.

Ramban repeated the statement that all of history is in the Song of Moses. In addition, Ramban challenged his gifted student to test him, and so he did.

The student asked the rabbi what his fate was in that passage. Ramban went a few feet from the student, Rabbi Abner, and said, "Go to Deuteronomy, Chapter 32, verse 26 and look at the 3rd letter of each word. There you will find your answer.

The verse Ramban directed Rabbi Abner to read was: "I thought I could make an end of them, I would make their memory cease from among men." Abner discovered his name in the Hebrew text. Distraught, Abner asked Ramban what was to become of him. Ramban quickly pointed out that that was only one way. Abner could choose another path where he would be a devoted disciple.

In yet another path, he would set out to sea without oarsmen or oar and never be seen again.

With the test successfully completed, Ramban proved the point and the absolute necessity that the Torah must be transcribed letter by letter. Even today, the Torah is reproduced precisely the same way, one letter at a time. Ramban also reminded his students of another important lesson handed down from generation to generation. "Should you perchance omit or add one single letter to the Torah, you would thereby destroy the universe."

This warning can also be found in the New Testament in Matthew 5:18: "I tell you the truth, until heaven and earth disappear, not the smallest letter, not the least stroke of a pen, will by any means disappear from the Law of Moses until everything is accomplished."

These verses obviously point to a waiting catastrophe should the Bible be manipulated. Today we've already seen Christian Bibles revised, rewritten and otherwise filled with all-inclusive language, including the changing of God's gender. Should some revisionists pen a new Torah, God forbid, or the last vestige of Christian Bibles such as the Douay-Rheims be changed, surely our era would end with a horrifying conclusion.

The study of the Bible Code is not something for only religious people. But, the code has had an intense affect on atheists, particularly scientists who had no use for God. Once these died in the wool atheists experienced the results of the Code, worked the math and proved their answers, they abandoned their atheistic beliefs and incorporated the Code into their work. Many scientists since examining the code have become deeply religious and now lecture about the complete union of science and religion. Jeffery Satinover, who wrote, *Cracking the Bible Code*, gave several examples of people who went through a major transformation.

One of those people was Eliyahu Rips, who was a "world-class" mathematician and a first-rate atheist. Rips is a group theorist, but after discovering the mathematical structures located in the Torah, including the codes, he became religious and eventually became an Orthodox Jew. He continues to baffle his former colleagues with his work on the Code.

There are scores of such cases and they continue to be reported. Still, there are some people who believe the code is evil. After diligent and thorough investigations into the Bible Code, and working with the results, I have not found one example that would indicate the code is evil. Something evil would not benefit from the Code results indicating that God is Truth. There are hundreds of other examples, which positively refute the naysayers. I am sure there will always be detractors. That is usually the case when something can have a positive impact and turn people back to God. It is the well-worn and tiresome argument from the dark side.

Yet, we hear claims of probability and chance. I have heard arguments during a myriad of radio shows. People claim that by using Moby Dick they could achieve the same results. Of course, those people wouldn't and more honestly, couldn't prove their statements.

We have witnessed over the last two hundred years a bashing by scientists of all things religious. Indeed, science has had religion on the run for some time. With countless theories and wonders, God and His laws of creation were relegated to the past. The future was bright, filled with the new laws of creation designed by Einstein and others. Thousands of inventions have made our everyday lives better. Cell phones, microwaves, computers and the Internet have become integral tools in our lives. However, God may have the last laugh because computers have brought about the cracking of the Bible Code in a monumental way. The last book that would be opened at the end of time, according to the prophet

Daniel, just might be the book of Life found in the Bible Code.

A curious blend of predestination and chance are both found in the Code. This parallel marriage is similar to quantum mechanics, which positions probability and statistics at the core of our existence. Free-will abounds in everything and history is the result of thousands of years of free choices. Interestingly, the Code reflects free will and has no set path that can be calculated. The Bible Code seems to incorporate dozens of different outcomes to every situation and in the end, I am sure the final trumpet blast can be found within the Torah.

The world as related by the Bible Code doesn't display a world that cannot change or that has a predetermined result. For instance, with every person in the Bible Code, as well as with every specific event, dates appear near the names, or targeted words. Birth dates, marriage dates, and even dates of death. Yet, finding the correct date may be difficult because of our free will and delayed mortality. Dates are shown, though, but trying to predict the actual date of a specific event is impossible. The Bible Code cannot be used as a glorified and highly sophisticated fortuneteller.

It is true that the dates could be laid out in a sort of probability curve, giving some outcomes statistically higher probabilities over others. Pairing names and events with dates is critical, but in that critical pairing, some couples would have completely insignificant meanings. Invariably, we end up with one date or another, one pair or another, with absolutely nothing located in between the two. It is an all or nothing deal. This, in a nutshell, reflects the probability curves in quantum mechanics and can also be found in ancient Jewish views. Satinover discusses Jewish prophecy as an "either or" situation with the thought that the Messiah will come to a good generation, one worthy of Him, or He will arrive in a completely unworthy generation.

There is no middle ground. In essence, we don't know things in advance using the Bible Code, but given enough information, we can discover things, crucial things, most of which are found ex post facto.

Even though things are discovered after the fact, doesn't negate the use of the Bible Code in research to verify certain events, deeds or misdeeds and to use the results to piece together the bigger picture.

With all the advances and truths revealed by quantum mechanics, we have been able to uncover all sorts of descriptions in and around our universe. However, we still do not know the true nature of the Creator who influences all of creation. To understand Him more fully, communication with Him is tantamount.

For religious persons, communicating with God has been a given. Moses was supplied with a bulk of communication, which helped him to know his Creator. In turn, Moses related that information to his people. Through the millennia, people have been known to turn off this communication with God, either through their own device or by the outside influences in our lives that try to drown out His voice. Except for devout people and the prophets, most of us just don't seem to communicate with God. Obviously, scientists want to know more about the laws that govern the universe, and on an individual basis, we each have issues that need clarification. God is just the one who can do that.

In ancient times, man possessed the wonderful grace of talking with God and hearing His voice, but through sin, that diminished. Perhaps with the Bible Code, we can become more familiar with Him and know Him as the God of Truth, Jesus as the Messiah, and God as the God of all mankind.

Using the Bible Code, I have correlated the rest of my research regarding the twisted roads that lead to Rome. At times, clues were given within the Bible Code that have helped to uncover diabolical practices and plans on the part of the New World Order. It has been an interesting, and, at times, a fatiguing journey, but one that has been worth it.

Each chapter will present different problems that we are facing now and where those problems will lead us. Particular citings from the Bible Code are presented which prove that God is talking to us, trying to help us, if we would only listen.

All of the codes used in this book were found using the software, Bible Codes Plus 2000.

As an example, please find below, God Encoded, God is Truth, and the Bible Code.

Found In Genesis 29:32

Found In Numbers 10:28

Code, Bible,Bible code
God
made
the
code
to
show
that
christ,jesus
is
Messiah

Chapter Two

When I first starting researching chemtrails and the other subjects for this book, I used the Bible Code. Sure enough, chemtrails appeared in the code and I have listed the partial findings in the book.

Before going into that, let's look at what contrails are and how they differ from the plethora of chemtrails that we are seeing in our skies.

Most people avoid looking up, as if the world above them didn't exist or as if it has no consequence. Law enforcement has known that this tendency is quite prevalent in human beings and has redesigned training to compensate for this flaw.

It was discovered during searches for suspects in houses and buildings that officers missed their suspect or were seriously wounded by the perpetrator who was hidden above them.

Today, being cognizant of all our surroundings is absolutely crucial. Although, most of us may not be involved with law enforcement pursuits, we do have a deadly criminal lurking above us. I am not the only one who has experienced the insidious anomalies. We have to recognize the present danger we are in and try to do something about it before we become statistics on the New World Order blotter.

In the past year, people from around the world have awakened to irregular activity in the skies. It is apparent, as technology has brought countries and people closer together; we have many things in common. This commonality is much more important than our differences. We are all targets of a dark agenda, an agenda that ultimately will result in a deadly outcome.

At a time when green candidates and proponents gripe about the thinning ozone, it is a wonder why those high profile people fail to mention the abundance of chemtrails deposited over most countries in the world. Surely, the very existence of millions of trails would alter the ozone and disrupt the already bizarre weather patterns.

There is something significant in the silence of the earth advocates. Is it possible that someone like Gore or Gorbachev or even Nader, along with their "green" gang just do not want us to know? Is the government doing something seriously harmful to the population?

I think once we give careful scrutiny to the evidence, we will conclude that, yes, they do know. Yes, the millions of chemtrails are hazardous, and, most definitely, they need to be stopped.

With over 62 million military and commercial flights a year in the United States, few people would be hard pressed to admit they have never seen a contrail. Jet aircraft exude a condensation vapor trail, which is apparent as the planes go above 10,000 feet. This is because of the thinning oxygen at higher altitudes. The vapor can be seen as a plane takes off and that vapor is quite dark. It resembles diesel exhaust from buses or semis. Once the jet passes the 10,000 feet mark, the contrails appear as white cloudy lines in the sky. This altitude mark is quite important to remember as we look at the facts surrounding chemtrails. For now, we will focus on the normal contrails.

Those contrails look like our breath on a cold winter morning. Just as our frosty breath hangs briefly in the air and then quickly dissipates, contrails normally disperse. The dissipation rate varies due to the prevailing winds aloft and their intensity.

The icy trails jets leave behind can form cirrus clouds. It is only natural then to assume with jet traffic nearing 100 million flights, that there would be an increase in cloud cover. According to NASA's Langley Research Center, cloud cover throughout the country has increased at least 5% in recent years.

To most pilots, this seems strange, because on a normal day, contrails are relatively short-lived. However, even the Geostationary Operational Satellites are detecting unusually long-lived contrails.

As exhaust from vehicles on the ground seems to create mass amounts of smog, it appears that contrails or what I believe are chemtrails, are trapping in heat over areas as great as tens of thousands of miles.

These contrail cloud formations tend to be seen in high traffic corridors over the country. Yet, recently, sparsely traveled skies developed the same cloud formation problems.

Overall, this abundance in cloud coverage may, by its warming nature, change our atmosphere considerably. An important note here is that although cloud formations are much more prevalent, the United States is in the midst of a formidable drought. Even the increased snowfall in the fall of 2000 may not be enough to alleviate the water table depletion.

Though "normal" contrails have become plentiful, they do not encompass the mass quantities of chemtrails seen all over the world. My research findings clearly show that contrails and chemtrails are not the same thing and they are only distantly related.

Whereas contrails should usually remain in the sky and form clouds when the relative humidity is above 60%, chemtrails seem to defy science. Just like the ones above my house that were produced in low humidity and were much too low to the ground. Chemtrails seem to develop and linger far beyond the reasonable life expectancy of a contrail. Further, chemtrails have appeared globally, with the exception of China and parts of Russia. They have appeared over parts of the world where jet traffic is at a minimum. Their appearances are also well under the 10,000 feet ceiling, where the oxygen and dirt levels are much thicker. With this in mind, contrails should not appear below that mandatory 10,000 feet level as thick white trails.

In addition, normal contrails run at particular altitudes east and west. They differ from the altitudes of flight corridors running north and south. These flight corridors were established for air safety and they are set in stone. These contrails in the corridors would rarely, if ever, form a checkerboard, lacing pattern or a giant X in the sky, to the extent that we see today. Such is not the case with the chemtrails, which have been observed. To have interwoven patterns or x's in the sky is abnormal. For example, please see the pictures on the following pages.

Those patterns go against regular air traffic control patterns. In fact, they challenge FAA flight safety rules. The only flights to supercede those rules would be government planes. You can bet the air traffic controllers know the planes, their flight paths and what they are doing 24 hours a day.

It has become apparent from eyewitness accounts, that several planes, all within a few hundred feet of one another are spraying certain areas of the country with a substance that could prove injurious to millions of people.

There is much speculation about the origins and the purpose behind the chemtrails. Some sources indicate that the Pentagon and other Federal agencies are testing anti-biological warfare agents. According to sources deep within the National Security Agency, (NSA) the government is utilizing Air Force and Air National Guard planes to accomplish this "testing."

The chemtrails, unlike contrails, spray out cloud formations in a line. Again, these formations are unheard of when the relative humidity is low.

Some NSA sources have indicated that Defense Advanced Research Projects Agency, or DARPA, has funded studies in anti-biological warfare. However, DARPA does not claim to be involved in the widespread spraying of chemtrails.

If you pay attention to the news, it is obvious that the US Government is bracing for a biological or chemical attack that is expected at any time.

Many countries, including Third World countries, are developing chemical and biological weapons, as well as Russia and China. Visionaries have warned us that the US is in particular danger of a massive biological attack. As we see growing anti-American sentiment from countries throughout the world, the foreign threat is very real. What about a domestic threat of biological or chemical warfare?

So far, the government claims that this massive spraying is in no way harmful to the human population. Contrary to these claims, the hard evidence indicates that unsafe results have developed.

In 1999 and again in 2000, the government has been concerned about a flu epidemic. Strangely, within six days of chemtrails sightings, outbreaks of flu-like symptoms sprung up, passing epidemic proportions. This is particularly the case in 2000 when the flu vaccine did not get to doctors offices and clinics in time.

Pennsylvania had crammed emergency rooms in January 2000. Most of the people treated were there for flu-like symptoms. Emergency room traffic had to be diverted to other hospitals because of the overcrowded conditions.

Perhaps the revealing statistics of only five pre-holiday flu cases were all that were reported. If we look at the possibility of chemtrails being the culprit for this widespread outbreak, it might be beneficial.

One man in the Philadelphia area reported chemtrails, which were discernable at 4:00 PM on January 2, 2000. He actually saw the planes and was able to photograph the planes as they sprayed.

Another report on the same afternoon from Westmoreland County came in around 4:30 PM from a woman who admitted seeing the chemtrails and the planes that were doing the spraying. She didn't take photos, but claims that the chemtrails were in X patterns.

This woman described a plane exuding two contrails. The color of the trails was a distinctive gray. Apparently, ten people in her family became quite ill with respiratory problems, which were resistant to antibiotics.

Even evidence of pneumonia outbreaks surfaced and coincided with the appearance of chemtrails. The most common symptoms associated with the trails are:

> *Headache*
> *Sore throat*
> *Congestion*
> *Disorientation*

Stiff neck
Stomach sickness
Rash or sores

So what exactly is being sprayed in our skies? Is it truly a test of biological deterrents or something else?

DARPA gave Maxygen a $6.7 million dollar grant for the development of "aerosolized vaccines." Currently, Maxygen has been working on an anti-biological agent incorporating the commonly used protease, "subtilism," in an aerosolized format. Subtilism is an enzyme quite commonly found in laundry detergents. It has the capacity to break down cell walls, forcing bacteria to explode or dissolve into a benign substance.

DARPA appears in the Bible Code and the results are below.

Found In Genesis 9:5

DARPA

military

department

defense

secret

plan

rogue

CIA

underworld

DARPA

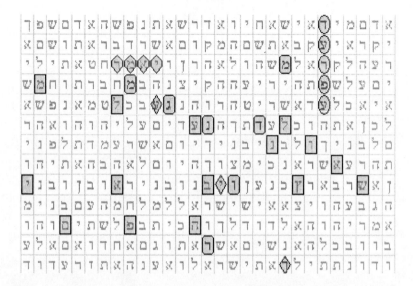

One theory as to the use of subtilism is that it could work in enzyme foam to be sprayed on affected individuals and decontaminate them. Since it would be nearly impossible to stop all biological or chemical attacks, the next best thing would be to establish counter measures that would lessen the blow of the attacking agent.

First, to be effective, a biological strike must come as a complete surprise, maximizing the number of victims. Therefore, trying to stop the rapid dispersal through means of gas masks and protective clothing would be impossible, especially in a civilian setting like New York City. Counter measures must already be in place for any hope of defense. The Unconventional Pathogen Countermeasures Program concentrates on the development of broad-spectrum, medical counter measures that would defeat pathogenic microorganisms or products. In order to accomplish this, the counter agent would have to be capable of stopping natural sources, engineered or manipulated agents without having to resort to individual agents targeted for specific threats, a task that would be too late to do any good.

So, the idea is to annihilate the pathogen's ability to enter the body and entering the bloodstream. Counter agents need to be developed that will be strong enough to be absorbed into the body effectively. It is also crucial that the right counter agents be found that would help the body's immune system fight the biological attack without having it overload the immune system.

Maxygen's main goal is to create decontamination reagents for Biological Warfare pathogens. The platform they are using is DNA shuffling. Shuffling is a revolutionary process for a guided evolution. That is all very technical and without a lot of study, is difficult to grasp.

Basically, in layman's terms, they are seeking to develop a defense against anthrax, botulism and other deadly biologicals. However, we must look at the fact that companies such as Maxygen could be developing offensive weapons as well or instead of the defensive mechanisms. Maxygen's own web page, *www.maxygen.com*, has references to their Advanced BioWarfare and Related Research.

Is the government experimenting on the general population? Perhaps the government is only trying to inoculate us against the risk of biological or chemical attacks. Certainly, the brouhaha over the anthrax vaccine in the military has become common knowledge, making many people leery of taking the vaccine.

Maybe the government is past the experimental stage and has moved on to an agenda that doesn't have the best interests of its citizens in mind.

Let's look at the words found in the Bible Code that are connected with chemtrails. The Bible Code cited that the word contrail came up twice. Words of particular interest are:

HIV
Methyl
Pandemic
Marker
Radium
Silencer
Styrax
Government
Scheme

Found In Exodus 1:22

CONTRAIL
HIV
methyl
pandemic
marker
radium
silencer
styrax
plane
government
scheme

Contrail

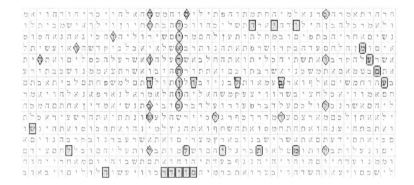

Note the word "marker." This marker could be used to identify the particular ingredients in a biological recipe. According to Will Thomas, an investigative journalist, this marker can be found in a coral reef in an ocean on the other side of the world.

Samples of chemtrails have shown bacterium, Pseudomonas Flouroscens, which is known for causing very serious blood infections. Will Thomas has noted this organism is cited in over 160 Pentagon Patents dealing with biological warfare applications. Pseudomonas Flouroscens is known to attack the respiratory system and is tied to severe coughing fits, vertigo, and general malaise. It is also antibiotic resistant.

With this evidence, it appears that the chemtrails may be more offensive than defensive in nature. There has been speculation as to the real purpose of the chemtrails:

1. *Weather modification*
2. *Mass depopulation or culling*
3. *Mass inoculation*

Having briefly touched upon the concept of weather modification and mass inoculation, let's look at mass depopulation or culling.

Our society is growing heavy with aging baby boomers. The graying of America is a well-known fact. Third World countries have exploding birth rates, which some sectors of society find intolerable. The UN, in particular, has spent millions of dollars trying to lower the world's birth rate through education, birth control and in some areas, promoting and funding sterilization.

Impoverished nations have long since been a drain on the UN coffers. It is probably safe to say that the New World Order crowd and the UN, in some cases, one in the same, believe survival of the fittest is in the world's best interest.

That could be why so many of the elderly succumb to pneumonia and flu-like maladies that accompany the chemtrails. Anyone with a weakened immune system would have difficulty in fighting the agents that attack them.

If you look at online weather sites, you can find pain and respiratory indices. Lately, those indices correlate with chemtrail spraying over the US. When the pain index is high and respiratory distress is up, chemtrails have been sprayed recently in those areas. Are the indices accurate or are they put up as a ruse to explain away the symptoms people have?

Many people who become ill with chemtrails have illnesses similar to Gulf War veterans. This could be indicative of biological warfare. It has been reported that Gulf War veterans and chemtrails victims test positive, (75-89%) for the pathogenic form of mycoplasma. This organism has many species, however, most of the people tested are found to have Mycoplasma Fermentans, (incognitus), Mycoplasma Penetrans, and Mycoplasma Pneumonia types.

These organisms are very slow growing and invade into deeper parts of the body, such as the lungs, heart, central nervous system, bone marrow, gastrointestinal, muscles, and joints. They can even invade the immune system and the brain. AIDS patients and Gulf War Syndrome patients have tested positive for these hard-to-treat organisms.

Long term antibiotic treatment lasting as long as two years has been found to be effective, but can be very hard on the body. Still, untreated infections with Mycoplasma can be much worse.

These organisms can be transmitted to others by coughing, sneezing, sharing food and drinks or in sexual contact.

Dr. Patricia Doyle wrote an open letter about an interview she had with John Middlebrook, Chief of Life Sciences at Dugway. She quoted Dr. Middlebrook as saying, "Dugway's chief enterprise is aerosolizing agents and in doing so, the issue of offensive vs. defensive research is seriously clouded.

"We have agricultural sprayers that make them, (aerosolized particles) the right size – half a micron is most effective... but those make them spray up and come right down. But, it doesn't take too much technology to make them stay up longer. With a good sprayer, we can cover 50-80 kilometers and still deliver infectious doses."

In an article I did for *The Messenger*, I discussed the concerns that the Pentagon has regarding what they view as a threat to this country. That concern centers on germ warfare, but not so much as it relates to cities. Rather, the Pentagon considers our ranch and farmland to be at greater risk.

The Pentagon published a report in January 2001 titled, "Proliferation: Threat and Response." In that report, the Pentagon said, "Attacks against US agricultural assets might be tempting, due to the perceived relative ease of attack."

Former Secretary of Defense, William Cohen, signed off on the report before leaving office. The report describes the various kinds of biological, chemical and other weapons of mass destruction, which pose a threat to the US. It further details the risk of the anthrax agent, which is debilitating and can cause deadly diseases in plants and animals. Foot and mouth disease is one of those devastating diseases.

In the fall of 2000, there were several cases of anthrax reported in the Dakotas, Nebraska, and Minnesota resulting in a significant number of cattle deaths. One family came down with the disease after eating beef that was contaminated with anthrax.

Drugs like erythromycin can fight anthrax and there is even an anthrax vaccine. However, many military personnel have resisted the vaccine due to its tendency to cause other more serious health problems. Some health officials believe that if you can tolerate the antibiotic, it might be wise to keep some on hand in case of an attack of anthrax. Yet, it may be difficult to diagnose in the early stages. If anthrax is inhaled, it can cause severe pneumonia and death.

"Also looming on the horizon is the prospect that these terror weapons will increasingly find their way into the hands of individuals and groups of fanatical terrorists or self-proclaimed apocalyptic prophets," the Pentagon report continued. Secretary Cohen added that Osama Bin Laden's men have already trained with toxic chemicals. There have been reports that he has men around the US in cell groups ready to release toxins onto the populace.

Bin Laden isn't the only one interested in deploying chemical or biological attacks against the US. Russia and China have been the main dealers in nuclear, biological and chemical weapons equipment along with technology. They have even "leased" their trained technicians to sympathetic countries.

You don't have to be a wealthy terrorist or nation to fund the purchase of anthrax. According to Patricia Doyle, "For exactly one US dollar, a terrorist can unleash a biological weapon of mass destruction capable of killing thousands of people."

Dr. Doyle continued, "Anthrax spores can be placed in breakable containers such as light bulbs and tossed onto subway tracks from the station or train."

Although some people, who have experienced chemtrails, claim that an insecticide or medicinal smell accompanies them, the latest chemtrails seem to produce no odor whatsoever.

An important point to consider is that bioweapons are tasteless, odorless and colorless. There is also a delay in the onset of symptoms, which can allow the terrorist activity to go undetected for several days. Of course, the current chemtrails allow a few days delay before symptoms appear. Just as with many biological weapons, the symptoms seem to be flu-like.

This chapter is not meant to be a definitive study of chemtrails, but rather an overview and food for thought that will, hopefully, motivate us to storm Washington and to demand answers.

There are many fine studies available on chemtrails and I encourage you to research them more extensively.

Below are prophecies, which relate to this particular road to Rome.

Veronica Lueken, a seer from Bayside, New York was given the following message:

> *"Did not My Mother pass along to you that knowledge that there would be diseases that your scientists will not be able to explain nor stop?" - Jesus, June 18, 1983*

Recently, a Midwestern visionary was given a message directly concerning chemtrails.

> *"...Have you found out about the planes flying over you with toxic chemicals?*

Have you checked your water supply lately?
Do you know how many foreign troops are
on your land and their purpose? These questions
are for all people in all countries, not just the
United States."

Chapter Three

On another thoroughfare headed towards Rome, one of the road signs reads: West Nile Virus Dead Ahead. We first heard about an outbreak of the West Nile Virus, or WNV back in 1999 when dead crows in New York City were found to have the virus. Since that time, there has been much speculation as to the origin of the virus and whether it has been responsible for any deaths on the eastern seaboard.

The West Nile Virus is a mosquito borne viral disease, which can cause swelling in the brain. Normally, WNV is found in West Asia, Africa, the Middle East and Europe.

You can acquire the disease from a bite of the northern house mosquito, Culex pepiens. So far, mild cases of WNV are asymptomatic. In the cases where there are symptoms, they may include: headache, fever, body aches, as well as skin rashes and swollen lymph glands.

In rare cases, more serous infections can occur. High fever, stiff neck, disorientation, coma, convulsions, paralysis and death are a few of the worst side effects. People who have contracted WNV aren't necessarily hospitalized. In most cases, a person recovers spontaneously. The more severe cases obviously require hospitalization. However, there is no specific therapy for the disease. Currently, several research labs are working on the solution.

Although New York City attributes seven deaths to WNV, there have only been 2 documented deaths that meet the criteria. The elderly seem most prone to the disease.

The Bible Code mentions West Nile and the findings are listed below.

Found in Leviticus 9:24

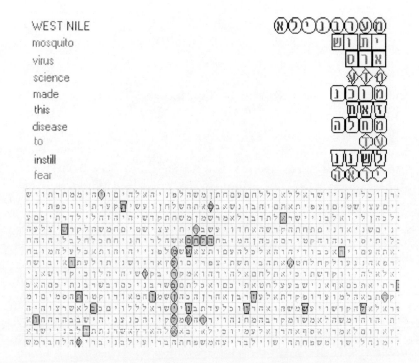

There is a common thread with WNV, anthrax, chemtrails and other biological attack methods. The CIA is connected to that dubious list. Their intentions could very well come down to global depopulation. The Bible Code has the CIA listed in innumerable matrices dealing with the end times.

So, it comes as no real surprise that they are involved with genetically engineered diseases. A fascinating aspect is that CIA is also tied to the malathione spraying in America's cities, which supposedly is designed to stop mosquitoes in their tracks. Malathione is a known human carcinogen and seems to do a better job at killing people than mosquitoes. Although, Mayor Guiliani insisted that the truck drivers spraying NYC and the various boroughs were not to wear protective masks. Even police acting as escorts for the sprayers were to drive with their car windows down and instructed not to wear masks. This was in an effort on the City's part to downplay any hazards to the population. Malathione is a close cousin to Agent Orange and it is known for destroying the immune system.

One of the giant potholes in this particular road is filled with sordid facts about the development and release of WNV in this country. Barricades and traffic cops re-route traffic away from the hole, but invariably, an investigator can manage to knock down a barricade and get a wheel stuck long enough to get a good look inside.

At the bottom of this pothole is not only a breeding ground for mosquitoes, but it is also the breeding ground from which secrets sprout. By shining a light at the bottom of this stinking hole, very well known snakes slither away to escape scrutiny.

Take a peak at one sizable snake: the US government. In December of 1990, the government called for the immediate development of West Nile Virus vaccine. Coincidentally, another brother snake opened a new pharmaceutical company in Cambridge, Massachusetts. It was called Oravax Company.

The vice president and head scientist is Colonel Thomas Monath, who prefers to be called Doctor Monath. The doctor is well versed in biowar research. He was a seasoned researcher at Fort Detrick's USAMRID biowar research program. Monath has been a crusader for BioWarfare preparedness and has been known to intensely push his ideas on former President Clinton.

He was a member of a special committee that advised Clinton on all aspects of biowar scenarios. One of his main goals was to stockpile tons of biowar vaccines. That is not a bad thing. It is a noble and a prudent goal.

However, that goal and the means to that end are anything but noble and not in the best interest of our country. Oravax set out in 1990 to win a contract from the Pentagon so they could make smallpox and other vaccines. The emerging multi-billion dollar market was ripe.

Oravax was not doing well by 1996. The vaccines it developed had not worked efficiently. Their stock price was down 90 percent from its initial offering. Yet, in 1996, Oravax was granted a license by the US Army BioWarfare lab at Fort Detrick to produce a vaccine for Japanese Encephalitis (JE). JE is derived from a genetically altered virus created by the US Army. A pertinent fact here is that West Nile Virus is a variation of JE.

According to sources, many scientists and physicians were experimenting with WNV in New York City and the surrounding areas for dozens of years. This research focused mainly on BioWarfare applications. Documentation exists which indicates that it was planned to release WNV on the entire US population. The WNV that was supposed to be released was genetically modified. From the press release issued on the vaccine, it said, "the construction of a chimeric virus in which the envelope genes of yellow fever vaccine are replaced with corresponding genes of the target WNV."

Because the vaccine is genetically altered, several problems have developed. Apparently, there is no way to know what harmful genes may have been added. In the arena of genetically modified food, for instance, researchers have found that bees that pollinate our plants end up incorporating the modified genes into their systems. That is why GM corn has not been fit for human consumption and that is especially true of genetically engineered oral vaccines.

New York City officials worked at showing New Yorkers that it was going to take WNV very seriously and started the massive spraying campaign. A red flag went up for many scientists who already knew that malathione isn't effective against mosquitoes. If anything, subsequent generations of mosquitoes become resistant to the toxin. Therefore, you end up with more and more mosquitoes that carry WNV, which obviously increases the spread of the disease.

What was Mayor Guiliani thinking? Evidence suggests he knew that the answer to an "engineered epidemic" would be the Oravax vaccine. One of Dr. Monath's associates on the WNV development project is Doctor Jerry Hauer. Hauer was the former head of the Office of Emergency Management for NYC and was a friend of Guiliani.

It is important to mention here that Doctor Hauer has been publicly outspoken for the need for a "real-life" simulation of a bioweapons attack. Several doctors from the scientific community believed that the development of the WNV vaccine was in the works and that the release of the virus on New Yorkers was intentional.

The connection with intense spraying, which does little in killing mosquitoes, but is extremely injurious to humans, was well thought out. With the spread of WNV, panic would set in and people would willingly swallow the vaccine, as its manufacturer reaped astronomical monetary gains. Yet, it is not entirely about the money. The billions that could be made are just bonus bucks for those involved in a more insidious global venture designed to accomplish global genocide.

When I first started my research about 20 years ago, I had discounted the Rockefeller connection to the New World Order. I quickly changed my mind as the evidence rolled in, proving their connection and their deadly plans.

Once again, the Rockefellers have been found to be part of engineered diseases even to the extent of using Rockefeller University in Manhattan to aid in their development.

So, while the doctors' and chief architects' bank accounts become morbidly obese with blood money, they are accomplishing their agenda for depopulation. Basically, the Haves get richer and the Have-Nots are eliminated, the consummate interpretation of survival of the fittest.

MOUSEPOX

Usually when the death toll of any busy highway gets too high, the road is overhauled and corrective measures are taken. If that doesn't substantially change the mortality rate, the road is closed.

That's not the case with Mousepox Disease. The mortality rate with this engineered illness is calculated to be between 80-100%, but rather than destroying the manual on how to create it, (it was supposedly created by accident) the people responsible told the world how to develop it.

Australian scientists inadvertently came up with what could turn out to be a rather efficient killer. Using technology that could be used in biological warfare, they created a killer mouse virus. In its mouse form, it is harmless to humans. However, there is a giant catch.

Inserting a gene that produces a molecule called interleukin 4 or IL-4, into a mouse virus that is similar to smallpox, creates the virus. That set the scientific community reeling in fear that a lethal human dose could be engineered.

"It would be safe to assume that if some idiot did put human IL-4 into human smallpox, they'd increase the lethality quite dramatically," said Ron Jackson, a scientist who helped to create the virus.

Throughout the scientific world, concerns have been raised for some time that terrorists would use scientific research to engineer killer viruses. Unfortunately, this latest incident out of Australia has proven those concerns to be valid.

Jackson contends that by telling the scientific community what had happened, that would warn them about potentially dangerous technology. Apparently, Jackson felt that his findings would deter scientists from similar projects. The scientific community on the other hand was appalled that the information was put out at all. Instead, it was felt that Jackson and his colleagues should have burned the data and kept quiet. By releasing excessive and deadly information, the blueprints for disaster could be copied and quickly put into use.

Given the psychological climate of the world today, there is no doubt someone is working on this new disease and will sell it to the highest bidder.

Nine days after the test mice were injected with the virus, all of the mice were dead. Part of their immune system had been wiped out. According to researchers, the vaccine that would have protected the mice against strains of the virus was only effective on 50 percent of the mice exposed to the new virus.

With slight modification, this virus could be used on different animals like sheep and cattle. It would be a very powerful and effective tool for terrorists who want to shut down an enemy's food supply.

SMALLPOX

We're not in good shape when it comes to smallpox. Children have not been vaccinated against it since 1977, leaving them and their children soft targets for a biological attack.

A secret federal assessment concludes that Iraq, North Korea and Russia are most likely concealing the smallpox virus for military use. A senior Soviet defector told US officials that blood samples of North Korean soldiers showed recent smallpox vaccinations, which are relatively uncommon.

He even listed Iraqi reports about the recent manufacturing of smallpox vaccine.

This information was a key point in President Clinton's decision not to destroy American supplies of the virus.

Smallpox was declared completely eradicated over 20 years ago. This leaves a question about whether our troops in Korea and near Iraq have received vaccinations for smallpox. Government officials say there doesn't seem to be an immediate threat involving the virus.

Smallpox is also known as variola. The virus is a super killer, which killed millions and crippled many survivors. The disease is extremely contagious. Variola is listed in the Bible Code and the results are shown below.

Found in Genesis 8:13

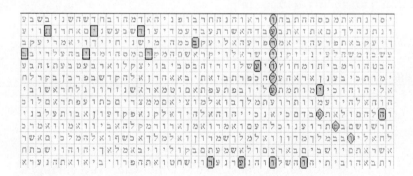

VARIOLA
future
problem
BIO
WAR
USA

The Pentagon is working on a program that would develop a new vaccine. However, they don't think it can be put into use before 2005. Allegedly, heaven has told many visionaries that we only have a handful of years left. Will the vaccine be in time?

Russia adamantly opposes the virus' destruction fueling fears of future terrorism. The smallpox virus thrives only in the human body outside of laboratory conditions. For that reason, countries from around the globe have urged complete destruction of the virus.

Ken Alibek, a Soviet defector, arrived in the US in 1992. He was a top official in the Soviet's illicit germ warfare program. Alibek has told US officials that Russia has grown vast quantities of the virus.

Considering Russia's chummy behavior with Cuba and Russia's generosity in supplying North Korea and Iraq with the virus, we may have a larger threat just 90 miles off the Florida coast than we imagined.

EBOLA

Air travel has brought exotic and deadly diseases into our reality; others are just a plane ride away from the States. One horrible disease that could eventually end up here is Ebola. There was a scare during the fall of 2000 when a man had returned to Wisconsin from a trip to Africa. The 26-year-old man died from a strange virus and public health officials were understandably worried. Although the news later reported that the man did not die from Ebola, officials at the CDC were alarmed.

Ebola hemorrhagic fever is a severe disease that often ends in death for humans and nonhuman primates. The disease was initially recognized in 1976. Ebola was named after a Congo river in Africa. It is one of two members of a family of RNA viruses called Filaviridae.

Although the exact origin of the disease is not known, researchers believe the virus is zoonotic or animal-borne and lives in an animal host indigenous to Africa. There is a similar host that is associated with the Ebola-Reston virus subtype. You may recall that was discovered in imported monkeys in Virginia. As far as we know, no cases have been reported in the United States yet.

Supposedly, it has not been determined how the virus first manifests itself in humans. The consensus is that a person comes in contact with an infected animal. Then the virus can be passed along in several ways.

A person can be exposed to the virus by coming into direct contact with blood and/or secretions of an infected person. Because of this, we see the virus quickly passed through family members. Coming into contact with needles contaminated by an infected person's blood is another way the disease can spread.

In laboratory situations, Ebola has been known to spread through airborne particles, but this has not been documented in real life situations involving humans.

Symptoms of the disease vary from person to person. Within a few days of infection, a person will exhibit a high fever, headache, muscle aches, stomach pain, fatigue and diarrhea. The man in Wisconsin reportedly had the same symptoms. Sore throat may be present along with hiccups, rash, red and itchy eyes, vomiting blood, and bloody diarrhea.

In approximately a week after being infected with the virus, chest pain occurs, shock and death ensues. Blindness and bleeding also accompany the disease.

At present, there is no standard treatment for Ebola HF. Supportive therapy consisting of balancing a patient's fluids and electrolytes, oxygen and treatment of any complicating infections are all that can be done.

In an outbreak of Ebola HF in the Congo, eight patients were given the blood of infected individuals who subsequently survived. Of those eight patients receiving treatments, seven survived. Due to the small nature of the study, the efficacy of the treatment is still unknown.

Ebola was found in the Bible Code and the results differ from the official reports.

Found In Exodus 1:5

OTHER HEMORRHAGIC DISEASES

The Arenaviridae familial group of viruses is associated with rodent-transmitted disease in humans.

Specific rodent hosts carry a particular relative of the virus. These viruses can be quite common in humans and are found in different parts of the world. They can cause severe illnesses.

In 1933, the first arenavirus, Lymphocytic Choimeningitis or LCMV, was isolated after an epidemic of St. Louis encephalitis. LCMV was discovered to be the cause of non-bacterial meningitis. New families of the arenavirus were found in the late 1950's and 1960's.

Arenaviruses can cause hemorrhagic disease. In 1969, the Lassa virus was responsible for an outbreak of human illness in Africa.

Like Ebola, the arenaviruses are zoonotic. Each virus is associated with a particular species of rodent. The disease does not seem to have much effect on the rodents and is passed along from the mother to her offspring in the Old World arenavirus. In the New World arenavirus, it can spread with bites.

Humans can become infected with the virus by coming in contact with excretions or material contaminated with excretions from an infected rodent. You can also acquire the disease by breathing in tiny particles that have been contaminated with urine or saliva of an infected rodent. We have already seen an outbreak in North America of Hanta virus, which spreads in the same way.

The Marburg hemorrhagic fever is rare, but a very serious type of hemorrhagic fever. It hits humans and nonhuman primates. It was first discovered in 1967 after an outbreak of hemorrhagic fever broke out concurrently in laboratories in Marburg and Frankfurt, Germany and Belgrade, Yugoslavia.

In total, 37 people became ill. They consisted of lab workers, medical personnel and family members. These patients had come into contact with African green monkeys. The Marburg virus is indigenous to Africa.

Humans can acquire the virus from animals, but then it can spread virally to other people as the cases in Europe have indicated. The symptoms of Marburg virus resemble diseases such as malaria or typhoid fever, making early diagnosis complicated.

The disease can be fatal in about 25 percent of the cases. Lingering effects of the disease make recovery tedious. There is no known specific treatment for the disease. Marburg comes up in the Bible Code and the results are listed below.

Found in Genesis 39:2

MARBURG
virus
blood
BIO
warfare
WILL
be
let
free
on
people

Terrorists wanting to hit their targets biologically have any number of diseases that can be utilized, engineered and transmitted with horrendous results.

Prophets have warned us that there would be severe plagues in the final days. We will be witnesses to some of the most destructive and hideous diseases in history. The Book of Revelation specifically mentions the plagues. Visionary messages are listed below that correlate with the Bible.

"The earth will be struck with plagues of all kinds; there will be wars up to the last war, which will then be waged by the ten kings of the Antichrist, kings who will all have a common design and will be the sole rulers of the world. Before this happens, there will be a sort of false peace in the world; people will think only of amusing themselves; the wicked will indulge in all kinds of sin; but the children of Holy Church, children of the true faith, my true imitators, will grow in the love of God and in the virtues dearest to me. Happy the humble souls lead by the Holy Ghost! I shall battle along with them until they reach the fullness of maturity."
–   Our Lady to Melanie of LaSalette – 19th century

"Jesus Christ will purify His people through cruel wars, famines, plagues, epidemics, and other horrible calamities. He will also afflict and weaken the Latin Church with many heresies. It is a period of defections, calamities and exterminations. Those Christians who survive the sword, plague and famines, will be few on earth."
- Venerable Bartholomew Holzshauser – 17th century

We may not all come in contact with hemorrhagic diseases, although the potential is certainly there. However, we will all be exposed to some genetic nightmares in the food we eat. The next chapter will deal with the possible orchestration and destruction of the food chain.

Chapter Four

It used to be there was nothing I liked better than a good steak. I live in the heart of the best beef country in the world. With the news of Mad Cow Disease spreading all over Europe and with a case in Louisiana, beef has been exiled from many homes. This particular road to Rome can destroy your nervous system while it steals the last bit of sanity before you die.

Of course, humans do not get Mad Cow disease. Instead, we contract nvCJD or new variant Creutzfeld-Jacob Disease. This hideous malady can lie dormant in your system for 10-20 years before waging a brutal war. Nothing can be done to help its victims.

Mad Cow disease or bovine spongiform encephalopathy, (BSE) is thought to have originated from scrapie, a prevalent spongiform encephalopathy found in sheep and goats. It was first observed in Europe during the mid-18th Century. The disease spread to most sheep-breeding countries and is quite common in the UK. The major increase of the disease, especially in the UK was attributed to feeding ruminants processed carcasses of livestock, including sheep. This was an acceptable practice and a good source of supplemental protein. Protein supplements were widely distributed to zoos, labs, breeding farms and regular households.

In 1980, rendering plants used different processing techniques, which may have triggered the problem. Originally, all parts of dead animals were boiled in large vats under high pressure. The newer process has left the agent for BSE in the bone meal without killing it. Contaminated supplements were then fed to previously healthy animals. Once they became ill or died, their infected carcasses kept the cycle going until outbreaks of the disease became rampant, as we are seeing in the past few years in Europe and is forecasted to hit the US.

The UK instituted defensive measures that were intended to break the vicious cycle of the disease. Other countries followed suit. A feed ban on ruminant protein feed was put into effect in 1988. Four years passed until the disease was somewhat under control. Yet, the losses in the beef industry were staggering in the UK. Over 200,000 diseased cattle died and an estimated 4.5 million asymptomatic cattle had to be destroyed.

This major blow to the cattle industry also hit other areas. Pharmaceuticals were hit hard because of the loss of bovine derived products. The tallow and gelatin industries were also victims.

Unfortunately, BSE has not been isolated in the UK. It is moving all over Europe at a steady rate, and could do the same in the United States. Due to imported live animals and the demand for imported food supplements, the disease seems to spread quickly.

No sooner had the early outbreak of BSE begun, when worry surfaced in medical communities about the spread of the disease in humans.

In 1990, the UK had a surveillance unit in place to monitor CJD. Other European countries added their monitors within three years. At the time, it was hoped that the surveillance could spot any change in the epidemiology of CJD.

When zoo ungulates along with domestic cats became infected, concerns mushroomed. The animals had all been fed supplement feed consisting of bone meal and uncooked tissue, which included various cattle parts, such as the brains. Now there was a lot of worry about humans who consumed beef and/or dairy products. Even ranchers, dairy farmers and butchers were thought to be at risk for the disease.

At first, these ideas were thrown out because it was believed that BSE originated from scrapie, which was not a human pathogen. Had there been a possibility that the pathogen could have been altered, thus possibly leaving people susceptible to the disease; the risk was deemed to be remote.

Human strains of CJD did not go to goats or to some rodents unless passed through cats or primates. The bovine strain of BSE didn't transmit to hamsters until it passed through mice. When the first 10 years passed after the original case of BSE was reported, and no higher rate of CJD was seen, there was hope that there was no relation to the bovine disease and human CJD.

All that changed in 1995, when three cases of CJD were reported to the surveillance team. The ages of the patients were surprisingly young: 16, 19 and 29 years of age. Following a neuropathic examination, it was learned that all of the three patients had amyloid plaques. That discovery was unanticipated. Normally, only 5-10% of sporadic cases of CJD displayed the amyloid plaques. The surveillance unit was quite concerned, particularly because of the ages of the victims. A new search was initialized to find similar patients who may have been misdiagnosed. Cases where sub acute sclerosing pan encephalitis, SSPE, was diagnosed were combed through largely in part because a monitoring unit in Poland found CJD in three patients who were found after SSPE monitoring.

Later in 1995, ten cases of CJD were detected in Great Britain. Of those ten, some had familial CJD or another disease. Those patients were over 50 years old. Two patients, ages 29 and 30, were discovered to have CJD. They had similar amyloid plaque buildup, as in the previous three cases. Now there was growing evidence that BSE was crossing over to humans, but physicians were reluctant to positively claim the correlation.

By January 1996, two more young patients were diagnosed with CJD. A distinct pattern was starting to emerge. Still, caution was stressed in the medical community. Another case was found in February of 1996, bringing the total to eight. Again, the plaque was present in this case, making it unanimous.

Genetic tests were run on six of the patients. Those test results showed no genetic cause for the disease. Then, the focus of investigation turned to geographic distribution. Two more cases arose in March 1996. It was then established that a new variant of CJD was occurring in people less than 45 years of age. It was then determined that the link was BSE.

Ominous laboratory results showed identical biological and molecular features from the BSE infected cattle cases and the human cases of nvCJD. Consumption of beef was the link and the source of the contamination. It was surmised that consumption of contaminated nervous system tissue was the villain.

Areas of contamination were thought to come from: cranial stunning instruments on killing rooms floors, contact of muscle with brain or spinal cord tissue, by saws or other tools used in the slaughter houses, and the inclusion of Paraspinal ganglia in cuts of meat containing vertebral tissue as in T-Bone steaks. Most important, meats like sausage or that used in beef pies and canned meats were thought to be suspect. Methods were put in place to lessen the contamination factor.

Depending on the amount of beef consumption is important, but genotypes in humans is just as significant. Caucasians may be more susceptible to infection because of this factor. Due to specific gene coding found in Caucasians, the infecting strain of BSE may have a higher impact than in non-Caucasians. It does not seem to be the case that Caucasians are in better socioeconomic positions and can eat more beef.

At the end of 2000, 87 definite cases of nvCJD in the UK were confirmed, and 1 or 2 cases in France and Ireland. The Irish victim had spent time in England. Although, in January 2001, an Irish farmer was overwhelmed when his herd was struck with BSE.

The European Union recently launched a "purchase for destruction" program that buys and incinerates up to 2 million head of cattle by the end of June 2001, costing member governments approximately $1 billion.

Due to the long incubation period of the disease, the possibility of spreading it from person to person is even greater. Infected blood donors might donate several pints of blood over the years and without stringent testing of the blood supply, thousands of people could contract the disease.

Already, we have seen patients contract CJD; some have acquired the disease through surgery. Although surgical instruments may have been sterilized, it has recently been learned that the sterilization process cannot kill the prion responsible. Subsequent surgical procedures, such as those in the UK, have led to more people contracting CJD.

Currently, several governments have policies in place designed to lessen the risk of transmission through blood donations. In the US, blood donor guidelines are laid down to prevent people from donating blood if they have visited the UK for six months or more during 1980-1996. Medical experts are also looking into dental procedures and disposable instruments to combat the problem.

Organ donors would also have to be thoroughly screened and as such, excluded if they are in a particular age group.

Another aspect of the transmission of the disease is the fact that sheep could be reinfected with the bovine adapted scrapie agent, making the sheep capable of infecting humans with the disease.

Mad Cow is listed in the Bible Code and the results are shown below.

Found in Numbers 9:5

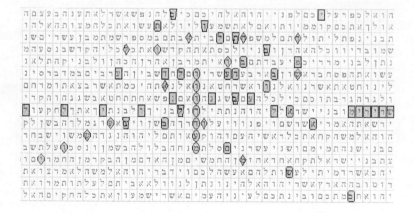

```
MAD COW
beef
disease
WILL
cross
over
to
people
made
in
a
LAB
come
to
THE
USA
```

Since there is no known treatment for CJD, it looms on the horizon as a most petrifying enemy. However, the governments and scientists around the world decide how to combat this loathsome killer will depend on how much economic damage will occur along with an increased death rate.

The Food and Agriculture Organization, (FAO) based in Rome, warned in January 2001 that Mad Cow could spread throughout the world. It urged governments to seriously evaluate the risks and take steps to prevent a human epidemic.

FAO, a UN agency, said, "There is an increasingly grave situation developing in the European Union, with BSE being identified in cattle in several member-states of the EU which have, until recently, been regarded as free from the disease."

Adamant, the FAO called for more extensive research to be conducted into the disease and the infectious agent along with its various modes of transmission. Currently, there is no human diagnostic method in the early stages of infection. There is no cure either for humans or animals.

Although the EU has made some effort to stop an epidemic, FAO said, "There is an urgent need to refine the risk assessment and to extend it to other countries and regions. Countries at risk should implement effective surveillance for BSE in cattle and controls in the animal feed and meat industries. At present, this means laboratory testing of samples from slaughtered cattle, and correct disposal of fallen stock and improved processing of offal and by-products."

Germany has had 19 cases of BSE as of January 2001 and immediately lowered the testing age for slaughtered animals from 30 month to 24 months. The EU's executive body has said that the infectious agent could only be detected after approximately a 3-5 year incubation period.

Certainly, it is prudent for testing, but it is also necessary to look at possible vectors for the disease to determine if there is another way BSE and TSE can spread. The culprit may not be only protein food supplements.

A report published in the December 4, 1999 Lancet made some interesting connections regarding fly larvae and pupae as vectors for scrapie.

The report stated that the team worked on an experimental means of transmission of the scrapie agent by flies. Since fly larvae eat meat, they were used in the study. Half of the larvae were fed with scrapie infected hamster brains that were in various stages of the disease. The other half was fed healthy brains.

After 14 days, larvae that died tested positive for the infectious prion. The control group of larvae was clear of the prion. The larvae that tested positive were then fed to hamsters.

Six of the eight hamsters that were orally inoculated with larvae got sick. Of those six, five tested positive. Two of the remaining four hamsters developed clinical signs of scrapie.

In another study done simultaneously with the larvae, were hay mites from farms where scrapie was present.

Hamsters who were inoculated with hay mites showed no clinical signs of scrapie. However, two of the four hamsters tested positive for the infectious agent after a very short incubation period.

The conclusion of the study was that larvae and pupae from flies that ate infectious hamster brains could indeed transmit scrapie. Transmission attempts using hay mites failed. The study suggested that the number of mites inoculated might have been too small. Researchers involved with the study felt that their results were relevant to the transmission of BSE. That brings a whole new set of problems in the eradication of the disease.

Reports from Western Kentucky bring another problem under scrutiny. Two neurologists from Kentucky published a paper in the August 1997 Lancet. Joseph Berger and Eric Weisman discovered a pattern. In the previous four years, five people in western Kentucky were diagnosed with CJD.

The common denominator is that all five patients consumed squirrel brains. The doctors concluded their paper by saying that "Caution might be exercised in the ingestion of this arboreal rodent." It is hard to imagine that anyone enjoys squirrel brains, but it is a savored delicacy in some parts of the US.

Eric Weisman said in his Lancet paper, "Someone comes by the house with just the head of a squirrel and gives it to the matriarch of the family. She shaves the fur off the top of the head and fries the head whole. The skull is cracked open at the dinner table and the brains are sucked out."

Stories about Mad Cow appeared in local papers. Some people stopped eating squirrel brains for the first time in decades. It wasn't long before Eric Weisman saw his first squirrel brain gourmand at Weisman's Neurobehavioral Institute. In 1993, a mayor of a small town in the area came in for check-up. At first, it was thought the 54-year-old man had a stroke. He hit a car because he couldn't see it coming at him on his left side. He was then fired from his sales job because he failed to fill out the left side of sales forms.

Eventually, he was diagnosed with non-dominant hemispheric syndrome. In other words, the left side of his world ceased to exist. The right side of the man's brain had atrophied. During the examination, Weisman saw the man jerk. Hans Creutzfeld had a patient who presented with the same symptom. He named the disease after himself and his colleague, Alfons Jakob.

Shortly after seeing Weisman, the mayor's mind started to deteriorate. He became violent. Complicated thought eluded him.

Other patients arrived at the Institute and they had similar symptoms. So, Weisman decided to conduct a survey. Checking his CJD records, he found 100 local people. Of those 100, 27 people had eaten squirrel brains.

Three million people hunt squirrels in America. In Kentucky, Ohio and Tennessee, twenty-five million squirrels are killed each year. With this information, Weisman figured that many more cases of CJD would develop.

After writing the paper for the Lancet. Weisman and Berger took a lot of criticism, mainly because squirrels were not known to carry CJD. The squirrel diet consists of fruits and nuts and they don't eat each other's brains. Yet, Weisman noted that city squirrels eat suet out of people's hands. The age of patients who had CJD was generally over 50. So, Weisman assumed that perhaps the squirrel population had an epidemic 30 years ago. That would account for the long-term incubation and age of the CJD patients.

Weisman decided to capture some squirrels and check them for CJD. He had difficulty in acquiring test subjects, partly because the locals thought he was a crazy Yankee with stupid ideas. Even though Weisman's wife grew up eating squirrel brains in Kentucky, it didn't help the situation.

After finally obtaining 50 squirrels and their necrotopsies were performed, none were found to carry the disease.

A few deer hunters have contracted CJD. Now, deer hunters are asked to turn in the brain stems of the deer they shoot for evaluation. Chronic Wasting Disease, the deer equivalent of Mad Cow, has moved through Wyoming and Colorado and is now in Nebraska. Untainted meat will be much harder to find in the end-times.

Recently, panic set-in among Germans due to the spread of Mad Cow Disease across Europe. Store shelves were bare and zookeepers turned to eating zoo animals rather than give up meat. Germany may be on the verge of martial law.

Strangely, Germany may have played a part in the development of BSE. One of the most recent reports has been the supposed relationship between insecticide and Mad Cow Disease. According to sources, the UK is ignoring new scientific research that indicates that the British fight against warble flies was responsible for triggering the upsurge in Mad Cow Disease.

Studies show that prions can bond with manganese in animal feeds, or in some instances, mineral licks. Manganese prions can cause neurological degeneration like that associated with BSE. Unpublished research reports conclude that Phosmet, a chemical insecticide produced by ICI, can damage prions, in the spines of cattle, along with insecticide application. ICI's Phosmet, organophosphate (OP) insecticide allegedly caused the damage.

Human brains can also suffer similar damage after applications of lice shampoo that contains organophosphates. Decades later, neurological diseases like CJD or Alzheimer's can develop.

With the UK leading the fight against protein supplements, the link to insecticides and BSE has been intentionally overlooked. Some scientists feel this is a real tragedy and investigations should be conducted immediately.

David R. Brown, a Cambridge University prion specialist, has conducted experiments that show manganese bonds in a damaging way with prions.

Nazi chemists originally developed organophosphates during World War II. However, they were used as chemical weapon nerve agents. It appears Germany's chickens have come home to roost.

Should more solid evidence emerge from this research, ICI could suffer heavy financial losses resulting from litigation brought by CJD patients and their families.

Unfortunately, this particular insecticide was not relegated only to the UK. In 1996, former ICI subsidiary,

Zeneca, sold the Phosmet patent to a Post Office Box company in Arizona called Gowan. This happened just one week before the British government admitted a link between BSE and CJD.

ICI is a very powerful agent and has effectively used their influence to turn the spotlight in another direction. They have blocked investigations into the link between their insecticide and BSE. Nevertheless, that did not deter Mark Purdey, a scientist and organic farmer, from providing evidence that the warble fly insecticide was the cause of the disease.

One scientist scoffed at Purdey's findings, dismissing them as garbage. It was later learned, though, that Dr. David Ray was receiving funding from ICI and most definitely suffered a momentary lack of judgment.

Others jumped in to help ICI to discredit Mark Purdey. Companies like Bayer, Monsanto, Novartis, Pfizer, Roche and Schering-Plough flexed their considerable muscles.

A peculiar appointment by the British government in 1999 awarded David Ray by giving him a seat on the Veterinary Products Committee, (VPC). It is the government agency that licenses animal medicines.

Purdy, on the other hand, has failed in his attempts to secure funding for his research, even though the Purdey/Brown chemical poisoning model matches the epidemiological spread of CJD clusters in humans. That model also predicts the incidence of BSE-type diseases in animals. The current UK model fits neither.

The Pharmaceutical companies involved with this cover-up are quite concerned that the source of BSE and CJD will expose their role in Alzheimer's. With the growing numbers of Alzheimer's cases around the world, BSE and CJD lawsuit awards would seem like pocket change.

It is important to note that two leading brain researchers, who worked on CJD and Alzheimer's, have died under suspicious circumstances in the past few years.

Here in the US, the EPA is conducting studies into Phosmet's safety. The CDC has performed experiments on mice that confirm the organophosphate risk.

BSE will continue to spread as long as the chemical cause is not banned from use. Still, France, now experiencing sweeping Mad Cow Disease, has chosen to swallow misinformation and has initiated a warble fly campaign using; you guessed it -- organophosphate insecticide.

The greater risk to humans right now is the application of lotions for scabies and head lice. However, if the insecticide usage continues, beef consumption will dwindle out of necessity. Now that Gowan has sold the insecticide to US farmers and ranchers, perhaps it won't be long before we could see a mass number of BSE cases and CJD in humans.

So, the intent, of some powerful pharmaceutical companies, to avoid litigation may have taken a criminal route. That route has kept them from litigation so far, at the cost of human lives and the destruction of the beef industry.

Initially, perhaps, the insecticide was merely a mistake. Now, though, with evidence that contradicts the major pharmaceutical findings, it looks more like a global plot designed to eradicate the food supply and curb the population.

One thing is certain for all of us. If this disease is not stopped, global panic will ensue as the food supplies dwindle. In the next chapter, we will see genetically modified foods are driving us on the road to famine, taking their place among contaminated ruminants. Hard times are just up the road.

Chapter Five

A new form of terrorism has developed that has already had devastating consequences. Recently, it was discovered that the Foot and Mouth Disease epidemic in the United Kingdom was more than likely a terrorist act. The FMD that was responsible for outbreak was unlike any FMD in the world. In fact, the disease may have been a hybrid virus stolen from a lab in the UK and distributed to various herds throughout the country causing catastrophic losses.

Foot and Mouth Disease, or aftosa, is a very contagious virus that strikes cattle, sheep, goats and swine. Even deer, antelope and other cloven-footed animals are at risk for this disease. Horses do not acquire FMD.

Normally, with the onset of FMD, fluid filled blisters or vesicles appear on the lips, and tongues of the animals as well as other areas of the body where the skin is particularly thin, such as between the toes or on teats and udders.

Foot and Mouth Disease has seven types of viruses that attack particular species in different degrees of severity. FMD can be spread through ingestion or inhalation. In 24-48 hours, the disease enters the bloodstream of the animal, producing a fever. At this stage of the disease, which can last up to 36 hours, the virus can be excreted in the urine, feces, and saliva or in the milk. The next stage of the disease is the time that blisters break out on the gums, tongue and lips of affected animals. Within 24 hours, those blisters burst. This causes extreme pain, raw tissue and incredible inflammation. It can take up to two weeks for the sores to heal. The majorities of animals stop eating solid food and are often lame from the blisters on their feet.

FMD leads to severe economic hardship for farmers. While in mild cases, there is only a 5% mortality rate, in deadlier forms; the virus can kill up to 50% of the time. As we have seen in the outbreak in the UK, the government didn't wait for the disease to kill. It stepped in and destroyed unprecedented numbers of animals.

Even in animals that survive, weight loss occurs and in milk producing animals, milk flow is reduced appreciably.

FMD can be found in Europe, Asia, Africa and South America. It is tremendously difficult to combat this virus due to its longevity. The disease can thrive for some time in air and in food. It can even lie dormant in hair or hides and is easily carried from place to place by foot.

Consequently, farms were under quarantine in the UK and travel was harshly restricted in an effort to keep the disease from spreading further. Total disinfection of the farm and farm equipment has to be done and the animal carcasses must be burned. The pyres on the nightly news were a sad testimony to the utter devastation of the disease.

Vaccines have been developed which can help epidemics, but they cannot eradicate the disease. The United States has not seen a major outbreak of FMD since 1929. US farmers and ranchers have gone on the record stating that they are not equipped to handle an outbreak of FMD. Concerns are growing over the likelihood of the virus reaching the US.

A government lab, at Porton Downs in the UK, apparently experienced the theft of a vial of FMD nearly two months before the first case of the disease was discovered.

Apparently, a routine audit alerted officials to the missing test tube.

The lab also has smallpox, TB, anthrax and Ebola viruses on site. Sources have said that officials think an animal rights group may be responsible for the theft. On the surface, that doesn't make sense. Animal rights activists aren't out to hurt animals, but advocate humane treatment for all animals.

It seems, to some sources, that people, who wanted to have a profound impact on the meat industry, and the food supply, perpetrated this brand of terrorism.

The first case of FMD was discovered on February 20th, 2001 on an Essex farm. However, reports from timber merchants claim the Ministry of Agriculture, Fisheries and Food contacted them in early February because the agency was trying to obtain wood for pyres.

Nick Brown, the Minister of Agriculture, said this solicitation was merely for, "regular contingency planning exercise." He has denied that the government had any knowledge of the disease prior to the first case reported in late February. There were even reports from Wales which indicated the presence of FMD in livestock as early as January, one month after the test tube of FMD was reported missing.

The Bible Code has FMD or aftosa, listed and the results are shown on the next page.

Found In Exodus 26:15

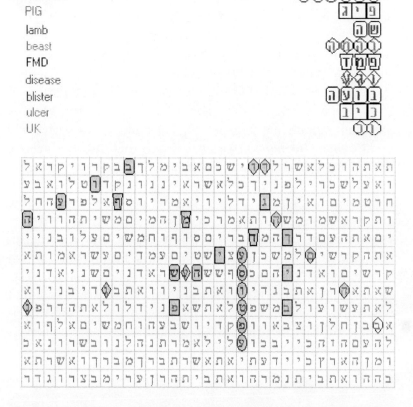

AFTOSA
PIG
lamb
beast
FMD
disease
blister
ulcer
UK

US officials are preparing for an outbreak of FMD and they consider the chances for seeing the disease here as quite likely. Officials from FEMA, CIA, FDA and the Department of Agriculture met in April 2001 to discuss plans for combating an epidemic.

One FEMA official, Bruce Baughman, stated that FMD would be handled the same as any other national disaster. Although government officials devoted their energies to keeping the disease from reaching the US, the focus has shifted to planning for the very real threat.

Plans for earthmoving equipment to be on hand to help bury carcasses have been put into effect. Emergency orders have been drafted allowing for the suspension of environmental regulations in case burial of the carcasses becomes necessary. Since the February outbreak in the UK, the US has added hundreds of inspectors at ports and airports in hopes of keeping the disease out of this country.

In Minnesota, state officials have considered asking the state legislature for the authority to declare martial law in case of an outbreak of FMD. Currently, a task force is studying the situation to see if emergency powers are adequate or if a new statute is required to handle the situation. Officials are now considering obtaining funds from the legislature in order to put contingency plans in place.

Practical aspects are also being weighed such as delivering groceries to farm families in case of an epidemic. This was also done in the UK. Approximately 30 states have joined Minnesota in planning for a possible outbreak.

Financial losses for farmers in the UK were staggering, driving some farmers to suicide. The government there contemplated gun confiscation to keep down the number of suicides.

Here in the US, Plum Island is home to test tubes of FMD, among other diseases mentioned in previous chapters. Considering the security problems in the UK, it gives one little comfort. Still, Peter Mason, head of the US Department of Agriculture's FMD research on Plum Island, said, "There are multiple layers of security to keep the virus from getting off the island." Plum Island is a former US Army base called Ft. Terry. Ft. Terry came up in the Bible Code and the results are on the next page.

Found In Genesis 41:13

Ft. Terry
plum
island
BIO
warfare
made
LYME
disease
west
NILE
to
make
people
sick
weakening
them
for
anti-
christ
and
U.N.
control

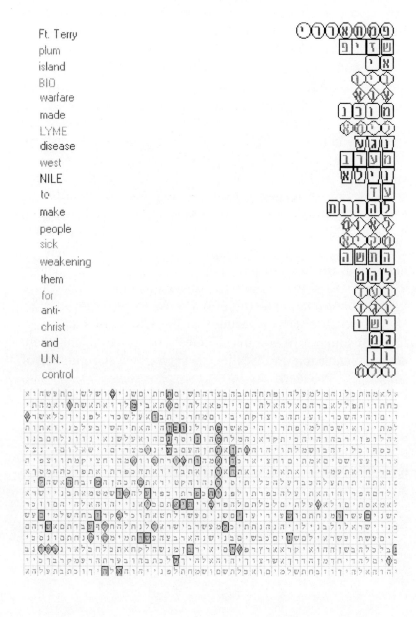

Tourism and globetrotting fuel the concerns of the US government about FMD. Importation of meat has been banned, but with FMD traveling in the soles of shoes, the possibility for contamination exists.

Although the disease isn't normally serious in humans, emanating toxins from the burning carcasses can be quite a health hazard. The UK government has admitted people who lived near the pyres could easily become sick. Smoke from the fires can worsen asthma and can expose people to harmful irritants like sulfur dioxide. There is also an economic impact with FMD that goes far beyond the farmers. Tourism has taken a dive since Mad Cow disease and FMD have broken out.

Yet, bio-terrorism is like an octopus stretching out its tentacles until it firmly grips the globe. Without proper precautions, the people behind this kind of war will no doubt inflict far more damage unless they are stopped. My sources claim that the people responsible for this kind of war will not stop until they achieve total control of the food industry, forcing their restrictions on what the world can or cannot eat. We are being driven down this dirt road into corrals where we will all be sorted. Many will be lost on this particular path to Rome.

Chapter Six

Genetically modified foods were supposed to be the road to the future. They were supposed to be draught resistant, pest resistant and hardier than any other crops. Instead, these highly evolved wonders are leaving people sick, and in some cases, hospitalization is required. Rather than enhancing our food stores for future hard times, the GM foods will ultimately be partly to blame for the coming worldwide famine. It could be that scientists have engineered a disaster that would force the unsuspecting into the hands of the Antichrist.

The general public grew quite fearful about genetically modified food in 2000. With a food scare that heightened those fears, evidence began to surface about the questionable safety of the food.

Britain, France and Sweden had a major problem develop in the spring of 2000 when it was learned that GM rape seed had been inadvertently planted. That seed had not been approved in Europe. Conventional seed was mixed with GM seed purchased from Advanta of Canada. Advanta stressed that the undesirable GM seed came from pollinated plants that were more than a kilometer away from the conventional seed crop.

At the same time, a disturbing discovery emerged in tests conducted by Genetic ID of Iowa. Over half of the samples of conventional seeds from American seed distributors had traces of GM seeds. Those traces can be caused by mixing seeds from various crops or by "gene-flow" cross-pollination.

September 2000 brought a huge scare to American consumers when Friends of the Earth concluded after testing, that GM maize intended only for animal use found its way into taco shells. The StarLink variety of corn was not approved for human consumption because it had a protein in it that could be a harsh allergen. Aventis CropScience makes StarLink.

A massive recall of hundreds of other items followed. Then in November, it was learned that the gene for StarLink protein might have crossed into other strains of maize. This didn't help corn exports and the financial outlook isn't good for many seed companies. One food company has strongly recommended that farmers not plant GM crops in 2001.

Some studies show no evidence that StarLink corn is harmful to humans. Somehow, the product found its way into the American diet. Watchdog groups are quite concerned, particularly because some modified crops are used to make drugs on a commercial scale. This new kind of "pharming" increases the chances that dangerous and possibly deadly mix-ups will occur.

There may be some hope according to a few British scientists who feel developing a plant that does not produce viable pollen could stop that gene flow. However, seed mix-ups are likely to keep occurring, unless separate mills are used for GM seed.

That may be small consolation to the victims who became ill. As of January 2001, 44 people have claimed that StarLink corn made them ill after eating food with bio-corn in it. Currently, the CDC is investigating claims made by people who may have consumed products containing Aventis SA's gene-spliced StarLink corn. Records show that the people suffered from diarrhea, vomiting, rashes, itching and anaphylactic shock.

The EPA is now considering if Aventis SA should be given temporary approval to use StarLink in human food. Serious liability issues could arise if the EPA restricts StarLink's use.

One man who ate corn chips went into anaphylactic shock. Although the man had no history of allergies, he found himself in the hospital. A 13-year-old boy was also admitted to a hospital when his face and tongue swelled after eating flour tortillas.

The data on StarLink and its side effects are sparse. Some groups are quite concerned that the corn is much too risky for human consumption. Aventis, on the other hand, doesn't feel that people could consume enough of the modified corn to present any health risk.

Of the 44 cases reported, 16% of the illnesses were deemed "unlikely" to be linked to food allergies related to StarLink.

I ran StarLink in the Bible Code and the results are listed below.

Found in Genesis 35:1

Starlink
corn
tainted
by
MEN
to
cause
sickness

Starlink

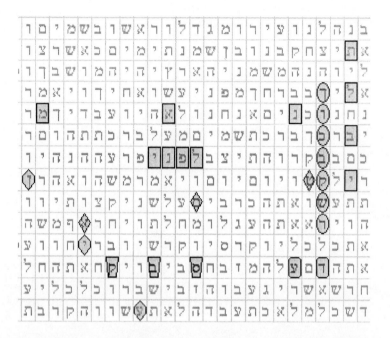

Carol Rubin, a veterinarian at the CDC, said that a highly specific laboratory test should be developed to determine if StarLink was responsible.

FDA data was analyzed by the CDC and found that only 11 people had allergic symptoms. An allergic case established by CDC criteria had to present itself within 12 hours of actual food consumption.

In researching this issue, I had to find out if the FDA regulated GM food. For over a decade, frankenfood has gone largely unregulated, which means we have all been human guinea pigs.

A Federal judge upheld the FDA's policy regarding genetically modified food. The judge's decision came on the heels of the taco shell scare. Dismissing the lawsuit over the tainted taco shells, the judge reaffirmed the 1992 FDA policy on GM foods, saying they were believed to be safe and would not be regulated as food additives. Further, labeling for GM foods would not be necessary since the food was not changed in a "material" way.

Former President Clinton, in a strange move that upset consumer and environmental groups, appointed a former Monsanto lobbyist to represent consumers on a transatlantic committee. This appointment was to help allay fears and to avoid a possible trade war over GM foods.

Hostilities arose between the US and Europe over GM foods and brought about a major conflict at the 1999 World Trade Organization, (WTO) in Seattle.

In May 2000, European and US leaders agreed to set-up a 20 person Biotechnology Consultative Forum that represents both sides of the fiery battle.

Former Secretary of State Madeline Albright wanted the US team to draft a compromise on labeling, safety testing and other regulatory problems. Albright also asked specific groups to nominate members for the team. However, those nominations were ignored and Carol Tucker Foreman got the assignment.

Foreman is a Capitol insider who lobbied for the GM food king, Monsanto. The company is also known for their bovine growth hormone additives that stimulate milk production.

Her defenders found it ridiculous that she would be still intimate with Monsanto. The big chicken farmers were thought to be very close to Foreman, especially Tyson Chicken, when the Arkansas native relaxed poultry inspection rules. Many of Foreman's detractors feel that her position would not be favorable to the consumer and that her allegiance was still to Monsanto.

The war over GM foods will likely continue despite consumer and some government efforts to stop its addition to food destined for human consumption.

Further, since many companies like Monsanto insist on selling seed to farmers that won't pollinate, the control over future corps lies completely with the companies and not the farmers. Control like that will lead to a worldwide famine. It could very well be a planned global famine.

In studying the evidence, it is quite obvious that there is a plan. Why would companies create a Terminator seed unless they wanted total control of the world's food supply? The Terminator seed guarantees that there will be no second-generation seed for planting the following season.

The cottonseed may offer the best illustration of this takeover plan. Normally, cotton is not sold as a hybrid seed. That makes it the ideal seed for Terminator protection. Other crops that do not use hybrid seeds are wheat, rice and soybeans. Corn is usually hybrid and farmers have to buy seed every year.

By not using hybrid crops, farmers avoid having to go back to the seed distributors for several years. This really hurts the bottom line of companies like Monsanto.

Money isn't the only motivation though. The Terminator may have been developed to kill the second-generation seed. With hybrids, the second generation is variable. The genes from the first generation are present in the second generation, though the combination of genes is unpredictable. Still, growers who want to grow their own seed could experiment with the second-generation seed and develop their own special seed. The Terminator destroys that generation entirely killing competition. It also kills any likelihood farmers would have seeds for the next season.

The Terminator has a very good chance of spreading to other plants, killing seeds and sowing destruction. Fields that may be next to Terminator fields will no doubt have toxic pollination due to the killer genes. Each grain of pollen will carry the toxin. We have to look at the impact on this killer as it relates to birds, insects and cattle that may forage in the fields after harvest.

There are also implications regarding the harm done to the soil.

Land prices may fall dramatically because of the use of GM crops. Great Britain is seeing this effect and it is akin to land that has been contaminated or diseased. No one wants to buy the land. There are no winners with GM seed except for the companies that developed them and eventually the Antichrist.

Terminator did not come up in the Bible code, but pollinate did with some interesting words listed below.

Found In Deuteronomy 6:10

pollinate
termination
corn
destroy
economy
start
famine

Should the global markers fail and financial institutions collapse, as prophecy has stated, farmers would most likely not have any way to finance their crops. The whole world would be on the verge of famine. Food stores around the world are nearly depleted right now and there aren't enough surpluses to see us through the famine.

One of the key elements that will elevate the Antichrist to power is famine. If these monster companies control the seed, they in effect, control the world.

Some examples of applicable prophecy are listed below with their sources.

> *"The trees shall not bear the usual quantity of fruit, fisheries shall become unproductive and the earth shall not yield its usual abundance. Inclement weather and famine shall come and fishes shall forsake the rivers. The people oppressed for want of food shall pine to death. Dreadful storms and hurricanes shall afflict them. Numberless diseases shall then prevail."*
> – St. Columbkille – 6th century

> *"Before the comet comes, many nations, the good excepted, will be scourged by want and famine. The great nation in the ocean that is inhabited by people of different tribes and descent will be devastated by earthquake, storm, and tidal wave. It will be divided and, in great part, submerged. That nation will also have many misfortunes at sea and lose its colonies."* – St. Hildegard – 12th century

"Before the war breaks out again, food will be scarce and expensive. There will be little work for the workers, and fathers will hear their children crying for food. There will be earthquakes and signs in the sun. Toward the end, darkness will cover the earth. When everyone believes that peace is ensured, when everyone least expects it, the great happening will begin. Revolution will break out in Italy almost at the same time as in France. For some time the Church will be without a Pope." – The Estatic of Tours – 19th century

"Woe, woe to man of earth. He calls down upon himself a just punishment for the abominations he commits in his heart and the abominations in the sacred temples of God.
Wars, famine, flood, cataclysm, and the Ball of Redemption. Know that in this order man shall be cleansed."
– Given to Veronica Lueken – May 30, 1974

Chapter Seven

Another serious problem to consider is the quality of water we have available. Pollution has certainly damaged our supply, but there are other problems potentially more dangerous.

For example, Red Tide is becoming wide spread and its consequences are formidable. It affects a part of our food supply and can cause illnesses and death in humans.

Water poisonings have increased dramatically since the 1970's. Studies have shown that the toxins produced by various single cell organisms can be lethal. One drop of water from an ocean, stream or pond can kill you if it contains certain organisms.

Since the mid 1980's, we've seen cattle drop dead from drinking pond water and people dying from eating mussels and assorted shellfish. Thousands of marine mammals have died.

Nearly every part of the world is affected by Red Tide. This anomaly forms when a concentration of microscopic algae is quite high. The algae then are quite dense and produce toxins that affects the central nervous system of fish. Death is the result. The levels of algae can be so thick as to change the water to red or brown. Green or blue algae also develop in the same way. Red Tide has a pronounced affect on fish, but not every species dies from it.

Often, fish die due to the lack of oxygen in the water. The smaller fish are the first to die off, decreasing the food supply for larger fish. When the die-off grows, the large species struggle to survive.

People are susceptible to Red Tide because the toxins can become airborne, resulting in respiratory distress, with throat, nose and eye irritation.

Eating shellfish that feed on the algae can result in neurotoxia shellfish poisoning or NSP. Symptoms can include nausea and dizziness that can last for several days.

Paralytic shellfish poisoning or PSP develops quickly, normally between one half hour to 2 hours after a person ingests shellfish. Complete respiratory paralysis can ensue in severe cases. Death follows if respiratory assistance is not provided. A person can recover from PSP usually within 12 hours if respiratory help is available. Normally, a person will recover completely. In extreme cases, death results from the collapse of the cardiovascular system. PSP can be acquired from eating mussels, clams, cockles and scallops.

A milder poisoning called Diarrheic shellfish poisoning or DSP appears within 30 minutes to 2-3 hours after eating shellfish. The subsequent illness can last for 3 days. Generally, the disease is non-life threatening. Eating mussels and scallops during Red Tide can cause the disease.

ASP or Amnesic Shellfish Poisoning is more serious. Gastrointestinal symptoms occur within 24 hours. This poisoning is very hard on elderly people. Symptoms are quite similar to Alzheimer's. Fatalities on record have all been among the elderly. ASP is acquired by eating mussels.

All people can suffer from shellfish poisoning. Statistics show, though, that tourists and the elderly are largely affected. Health officials think this is because quarantine notices and Red Tide warnings go unheeded.

Red Tide is not a new problem. History indicates that the anomaly is thousands of years old.

Some records show that the Red Sea may have been named because of the large accumulation of red algae. This may also be the reason that Jewish law forbade Jews to eat shellfish.

In recent history, shellfish poisoning was reported in 1793 when members of George Vancouver's crew became sick after dining on mussels harvested just off the coast of British Columbia.

Millions of dollars have been spent trying to find and isolate specific causes. So far, there has been little success.

Some scientists think pollution and sewage runoff might be a problem. Not all scientists are convinced of that fact yet. Reports of substantial pollution often do not have any development of algae in the water.

Another group of scientists think that ship ballast may be to blame. Ballast is the contaminated ship water that is taken on in one area and dumped in another.

The one thing that most scientists can agree on is that the study of Red Tide is very difficult. Below are the results from the Bible Code on Red Tide.

Found In Exodus 4:25

RED TIDE
algae
killing
fish
and
people

Red Tide

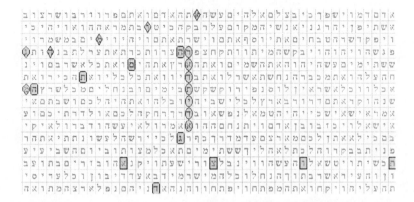

Frequently, we see man's intervention in ecology creating more of a problem than the original dilemma. So, research and progress are a trial and error situation.

Brown tides are the result of similar algae growth but no toxin is produced. However, the ecosystem takes a hit because of the shading problem and other side effects of high algae growth.

In the case of these tides, tens to hundreds of miles of coastline develop swaths of algae. Sea grass levels diminish with the low oxygen levels resulting from the copious algae.

Current flows have also been considered as a source or catalyst for the algae growth, but again, very few scientists seem to concur.

With harder times and less food on the shelves, using shellfish to supplement our diets may have severe repercussions. Even if you don't live near an ocean, streams, rivers and ponds may have their own set of problems.

We are seeing fresh water fish dying off in what was thought to be clear streams. For instance, trout in Wyoming have become sick with whirling disease. Whirling and trout come up in the Bible Code. The results are on the next page.

Found in Leviticus 11:26

whirling
trout
River
disease
brain
plan
to
remove
food
supply

Whirling Disease is one that attacks Salmonid fish such as trout, salmon and whitefish. The disease is caused by a microscopic parasite called Myxobolus Cerebralis. A glimpse at the life cycle of this miniscule parasite is complex. It involves two hosts. One host is a worm that makes its home at the bottom of streams and bodies of water. The parasite emerges from the worm and searches for a host fish. Once a fish is found, the parasite attaches itself, penetrating the skin. Eventually, it burrows into the cartilage of the fish, and then matures into a whirling disease spore. It lives off the fish until the fish dies.

During its life cycle, it sends spores into the water, which are eaten by worms. The cycle perpetuates itself.

The parasite causes nerve damage to the fish and also damages the cartilage. Infected fish chase their tails, creating a whirling motion. Fish may also develop black tails if they are young. Older fish contract odd deformities of the body and head.

Interestingly, the parasite is not indigenous to the United States. It originated in Europe and has been seen in Russia, South Africa, and New Zealand. However, that didn't stop the parasite from mysteriously showing up in the US. In 1956, it was found in Pennsylvania. Currently, over 22 states have reported the parasite's presence: Alabama, California, Colorado, Connecticut, Idaho, Maryland, Massachusetts, Michigan, Montana, Nevada, New Hampshire, New Jersey, New Mexico, New York, Ohio, Oregon, Pennsylvania, Utah, Virginia, Washington, West Virginia and Wyoming. Some of the states have had isolated cases of whirling disease, but in Montana and Colorado, the trout population has been hit extremely hard.

The parasite has been found on both sides of the Continental Divide. Effects of the disease seem to differ with different waters. Some have moderate problems, while others apparently have quite severe problems.

Humans do not have to worry about acquiring whirling disease. Still, the food supply of fresh water trout is in great jeopardy.

Any specie of trout and salmon can be infected. Although, that does not mean they will always develop the disease. Fish over four months old don't seem to have problems with whirling disease, but the young fish do. Hatcheries have epidemics that can wipe out their entire crop. Of all the species, Rainbow trout are much more prone to the disease. Brown trout have displayed a resistance to the parasite.

The State of Montana has reported infected species that have susceptibility to whirling disease:

Rainbow trout are susceptible
Bull trout and brown trout are partially susceptible
Chinook salmon are very susceptible
Coho salmon are quite resistant
Grayling are very resistant
Yellowstone and Westslope Cutthroat are susceptible
Mountain Whitefish and brook trout are susceptible

A single fish can literally be infected by over a million spores. This makes infected fish the most deadly source of infection.

Some researchers consider birds as possible vectors for the disease. Studies indicate the parasite can pass through a bird's digestive tract and still be infective to fish. A mature spore is quite healthy and can live for years in mud and water.

There is no known cure for whirling disease. Fisheries are trying to combat the disease so that it doesn't wipe out all the fish.

Important research has surfaced relating to Whirling Disease. Every state that has reported Whirling disease in epidemic numbers is also having major problems with Mad Deer and Mad Elk Disease. Further, states having large numbers of chemtrails also have Mad Deer, Mad Elk and Whirling Disease. I think there may be a connection and I don't think it stops with the deer and the trout.

In December 2000, the New Jersey Division of Fish and Wildlife recommended that hunters avoid shooting Atlantic Brant geese and warned them about handling or consuming them.

Nearly 700 Atlantic Brant geese died and were collected from the Brigantine Unit of the Forsythe National Wildlife

Wildlife Refuge. The geese were to be examined for the cause of the die-off.

The State Environmental Protection Commission urged hunters to keep away from geese that were exhibiting strange or abnormal behavior. Preliminary tests for bacteria came back negative, but more tests are still being conducted to determine the cause of death.

The Atlantic Brant is a small maritime goose that breeds in the Canadian Arctic, but winters along the Atlantic Coast. The latest figures show that 75 percent of the geese winter in New Jersey.

A second die-off that started in January 2001 saw 643 dead birds within six days. Both die-offs are thought to be related. Starvation is not the cause of death.

The birds apparently die quickly, often in mid-flight. Some of the birds have hemorrhaged hearts and some have spotted livers. Scientists have ruled out enteritis, contaminants and bacteria.

Generally, the birds seem to be in fairly good condition. Although, pulmonary edema and/or dark, wet lungs were seen in most of the birds. Blood vessels located in the brain, liver, lungs and kidneys were often congested with blood.

Tests for West Nile, duck plague, Newcastle disease and avian influenza have all been negative. Even tests for botulinum toxins and rodenticides were negative.

Oddly, many different species of birds frequent the Atlantic coastal area, but so far, only the Brant have been affected. Tests are still being conducted for infectious diseases and toxins.

At this point, it wasn't surprising to pull up Geese and Brant in the Bible Code. The results are on the next page.

Found in Genesis 11:19

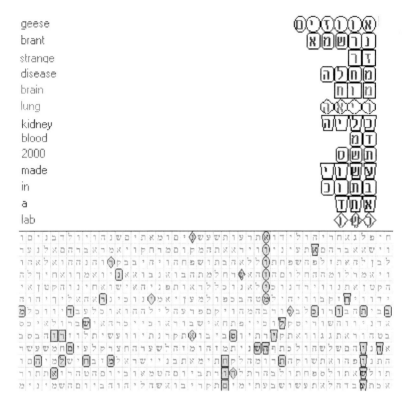

geese
brant
strange
disease
brain
lung
kidney
blood
2000
made
in
a
lab

New Jersey and the Atlantic coast are not alone in bird die-offs. Florida is experiencing the same problem, but it also seems to be affecting alligators.

A mysterious bacterium is showing up in Florida lakes. Right now, it hasn't been determined if the bacterium is harmful to humans. Yet, this bacterium is suspected in alligator and bird deaths in the area.

Over 150 alligators in the last 2 years have died from toxic algae. These algae previously found in Texas, Minnesota, and Kansas have now appeared in several Florida lakes.

The symptoms the birds and alligators exhibit are nearly the same: lethargic behavior, convulsions and death. Concerned scientists think that if the algae aren't responsible, then pesticides or an unknown virus is to blame. Currently, no public swimming beaches are open at Lake Griffin. The water quality has deteriorated so badly, that visitors to the area are down.

Captive alligators aren't having any better luck in Florida. Necropsies have revealed a new Mycoplasma bacteria has been isolated as the perpetrator in the deaths of captive alligators. It is likely that up to 1.5 million wild alligators may also be susceptible. Normally, alligators are hardy, resilient creatures, but this virus is proving to be a grave threat.

The infected alligators float in water for days without attempting to eat or to move. Alligators usually have a long life span, lasting eighty years or more. It has been exceptional to see dead adult alligators.

Upon examination of the reptiles at Lake Griffin, several were found to have microscopic sores in one portion of the brain. That area of the brain, about the size of the head of match, is responsible for the visual signals. Alligators with the virus can see but they can't make their muscles respond. Signals are slowed from the brain to the limbs due to the lesions on the brain.

Florida comes up once in the Bible Code and, you guessed it, it was listed with the alligators. Turtles are also mentioned in this particular code. Reports of turtle die-offs are also becoming numerous. This disease also killed over 45 endangered turtles. The results are on the next page.

Found in Deuteronomy 1:34

Florida
alligator
sickness
turtle
poison
water

Besides the strange bacteria in US waters, now we are seeing high arsenic concentrations in our ground water. Perhaps due to up flow of geothermal water, the dissolution of iron oxide and the dissolution of sulfide minerals, arsenic is becoming a crisis. Areas of Michigan, Minnesota, South Dakota, Oklahoma, Wisconsin, and Maine are seeing much higher levels of arsenic.

The EPA is seeking to reduce limits for arsenic in drinking water to one-tenth of the current standard in hopes of lowering cancer risks. The agency wants to lower the arsenic levels allowed from 50 parts per billion to 5 parts per billion. Currently, 6600 water plants across the United States would have to be upgraded.

Those plants serve 22.5 million people. Water industry officials said consumers would see at least a $100 per year increase in their water bills.

A new rule is to be put into effect in 2001. If the rule is adopted, any plant serving 10,000 people or more will have three years to make improvements. Smaller plants would have 5 years to comply. Industry representatives agree that arsenic levels are too high, but they prefer the World Health Organization's recommendation of 10 parts per billion. The National Academy of Sciences reported in 1999, arsenic in drinking water causes bladder, lung, skin cancer and could cause kidney and liver cancer.

Inorganic arsenic, the form attributed to cancer, is found naturally in the ground and is released into ground water that travels through the soil and rocks. Arsenic and water are found together in the Bible Code. The results are listed below.

Found in Deuteronomy 38:4

arsenic
in
water
US
plot
to
kill

Arsenic

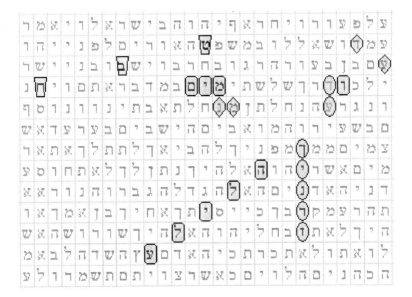

As we move into more treacherous times, animals and man will have a dire time with tainted water. Massive droughts are also expected. The results are obvious and there is little to be done without taking the necessary precautions to decontaminate the available water supply. It is also recommended to store water now before the quality deteriorates any further and before the quantity becomes scarce.

Chapter Eight

Law enforcement is changing worldwide. Some not so subtle changes are taking place in the US and even local police departments think the latest innovations are criminal. In January 2001, the Fraternal Order of Police had filed suit in Federal District Court challenging the US Department of Justice's policy of consent decrees to take over local police departments.

The Department of Justice, (DOJ) has already filed suit in Pittsburgh, Steubenville, Ohio, and Columbus, Ohio trying to take over those police departments.

Lately, the DOJ has targeted Buffalo, New York, Charleston, West Virginia, Eastpointe, Michigan, Los Angeles, New Orleans, New York City, Orange County, Florida, Prince George County, Maryland, Riverside, California, and Washington, D.C.

Local laws and applicable rules that relate to police training, policy and discipline are being ignored by the DOJ. Clearly, the FOP thinks this move is unconstitutional. That is one of the reasons the FOP is suing former US Attorney General Janet Reno and the US government.

The suit further challenges the exclusion of local law enforcement officers in the debate over the sweeping reforms. In many cities, this goes against collective bargaining agreements.

Other local police officers are quite concerned that the national police force will take over in this country and that ultimately, all police, here in the US and those around the world, will answer to the UN.

Should the FOP fail to fend off the Feds, local law enforcement will not be the same. In the US, we will lose substantial freedoms as the UN imposes its laws. Once those freedoms are gone, we can be assured they can never be recovered.

Europe is pushing for a rapid response force for "particular" police actions on the continent. This is above the NATO deployment and the goal is for at least a 60,000-man army. The purpose of this army is to be able to rapidly respond to situations as in Kosovo. More accurate numbers put the size of the force at 100,000 with 400 aircraft and 100 ships.

Britain and Germany said that the European Union Army would not weaken NATO. Although the draft communiqué called this force rapid deployment troops, conveying that people should not think of the troops as a EU army. The communiqué may not call the force an army but the Bible Code does and the results are listed below.

Found In Leviticus 11:4

EU ARMY
take
over
NATO
plan
rapid
action
force

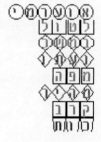

EU Army

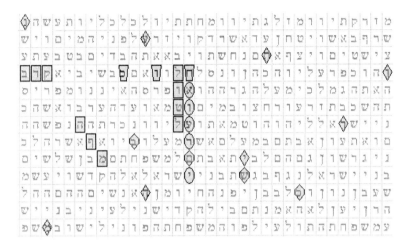

According to EU sources, the "army" would not be a standing army, rather one that is gathered in times of crisis.

Former Secretary of Defense, William Cohen, had serious concerns regarding the rapid deployment force saying, "if... they try to or are desirous of a separate operational planning capability, separate and distinct from NATO itself, then that is going to weaken ties between the US and NATO and NATO and the EU."

The rapid action deployment force would lessen the US role in situations like Kosovo where the US bore most of the responsibility. However, the EU force is moving into a more international police force climate, one which Kofi Annan, UN Secretary General, finds agreeable. He also wants to establish a UN rapid deployment force for similar crisis situations.

One of the more blatant moves, though, comes with the establishment of the International Criminal Court. First established in July 1998, 160 nations thought the legal barriers between countries should be dissolved, which eventually will hasten the final implementation of the New World Order.

Primarily, the ICC was formed to handle genocide, war crimes and crimes against humanity.

Kofi Annan described the ICC as "a giant step forward in the march towards human rights and the rule of law." It is a giant leap forward all right, a leap designed to strip us of our remaining rights. ICC opponents agree, feeling that national sovereignty is in jeopardy.

An International Criminal Court is not a new concept. The UN first saw the need for a court in 1948. With recent events in Kosovo, Bosnia and Rwanda, the UN Security Council pushed the formation of the ICC harder than ever.

The Seat of the Court will be in The Hague in the Netherlands. It will also hear cases in other venues as well. The court will hear cases in addition to the ones listed above such as endangerment, rape, torture, forced pregnancy, persecution on racial, ethnic or religious grounds and enforced disappearance.

Rome has asked the UN to include crimes of aggression, but a final definition was not resolved. A review conference will be formed to determine the exact meaning of crimes of aggression and then the court will hear those cases related to it.

Terrorism and drug crimes were also brought up for the ICC consideration, but again, the definitions were not satisfactorily met.

According to the UN, national courts will always have jurisdiction. So far, the ICC will only step in when national courts are "unable or unwilling" to handle specific cases. The ICC will knock down barriers established by certain countries that may have difficulty in prosecuting their own people. Supposedly, the ICC will only step in and deal with disputes between states and not with criminal acts committed by individuals.

A court prosecutor can begin investigations on crimes that are brought to that office's attention. There are also checks and balances in place that would prevent a prosecutor from starting an investigation without permission from a pre-trial chamber of three judges.

The States and the suspects can challenge the Prosecutor's right to investigate. Currently, the Prosecutor has to defer to states that want to handle particular cases on their own. The Security Council can also ask the Court to defer investigation or prosecution.

Prosecutors will be able to issue international arrest warrants. Under the ICC statute, in Chapter VII of the UN Charter, the enforcement of the Council's powers is binding on all countries. The court then can ask the Security Council to use its power to "compel" cooperation. This is further proof that national boundaries and laws are disintegrating, burned by a fire set by the UN. Extraditions, even from countries whose laws prevent extradition, would return suspects to the court. Many countries have indicated they are now willing to change their laws to comply with the court.

Countries who did not agree to be part of this new international community can have their citizens prosecuted by the court. Currently, states have seven years to change their laws to conform to the international statute.

President Clinton signed our national laws away right before he left office, guaranteeing our participation in the International Court. In some terrorist cases, the ICC may be a good idea, but we need to look at the court's ultimate potential to see where this may be taking us. The UN's new Charter has some very interesting laws that will affect us as individuals and not simply as nations.

The International Criminal Court appears in the Bible Code and the results are on the next page.

Found In 42:1

international
criminal
court
world
order
made
by
THE
ANTI
christ

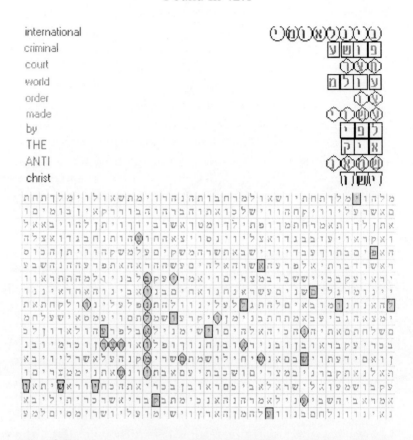

The following examples of the new laws clearly indicate the direction the UN is taking and where that leaves us. Initially, the International law may seem painless, but as time elapses, an international round up of supposed "criminals" is quite likely. Prophecy predicts the round up and as we review the new laws, it will become more apparent.

Let's look at Article 29 of the UN Charter to which Clinton made us subject:

1. **Everyone has duties to the community in which alone the free and full development of his personality is possible.**
2. **In the exercise of his rights and freedoms, everyone shall be subject only to such limitations as are determined by law solely for the purpose of securing due recognition and respect for the rights and freedoms of others and of meeting the just requirements of morality, public order and the general welfare in a democratic society.**
3. **These rights and freedoms may in no case be exercised contrary to the purposes and principles of the United Nations.**

On the surface, these items may seem benign. Yet, as the third article obviously points out, if the UN doesn't like you, your occupation or whatever is contrary to the UN, you are breaking the law.

Freedom of the press, freedom of expression and eventually, personal freedom will be null and void. Authors won't get published. Only acceptable news will be aired and so forth.

In the end, it will also include religious freedom. The UN is working very hard with the United Religions Initiative to make sure that all religions come under one fold, one doctrine and one leader.

Very few people are aware of just how far this has already gone. With Clinton signing the deal and Colin Powell now advising President Bush that a deal is a deal, there is no escape from UN control. It is only a matter of time before the Antichrist will be given total control over those of us who allow it.

I heard a radio talk show host say recently that the Antichrist was a scapegoat thing.

He said that Christians and fearful people need someone to
blame, that we're not being taken over by the UN and that
Armageddon is a fairy tale. I don't know where that host has
been hiding, but he's not living in the real world. The next
chapter will illustrate just how close to the final days we are.

Chapter Nine

Mikhail Gorbachev is a key player in the end-time games. Through his United Religions Initiative and State of the World Forum, Gorbachev is controlling massive pieces of a perilous puzzle. He and his friends hope that the few remaining pieces of our future remain incomprehensible until the last possible moment.

Under the guise of the "global good rooted in shared spiritual values," the URI is metastasizing to every corner and crack on the earth in hopes of uniting the world and developing respect and tolerance for all peoples. However, what Gorbachev and his group are really peddling is nothing short of the New World Order, calculated to strip us of our individual rights.

In the preamble of the URI, it states, "we respect the uniqueness of each tradition, and differences of practice or belief." Yet, as we have seen in the previous chapter on the UN, if those traditions are deemed "harmful," offenders will be brought before the International Court. So, what is the truth? Are we free to be unique individuals only until that exceptionality rubs those in power the wrong way?

We have already seen within the UN and its published documents that Christianity is acceptable only to a degree. Within the walls of the UN, the Antichrist and his organization are working hard to destroy the reputations of

Christians. In a mix of the world's religions, the Antichrist has managed to cultivate a hybrid religion, which in due course will become the only acceptable faith on the planet. Gorbachev and his pantheistic views are aligned with the Antichrist. It doesn't stop there.

Through URI, business leaders have been recruited to join this suspect country club and to instill in their companies the URI dogma, which goes hand in hand with the new UN human rights program. With that program adopted by businesses all over the world, it is easy to see where this will lead.

If workers fail to abide by this global charter, they will find themselves without jobs. Although that seems quite intolerant of individuals, it really fits right in line with the mysterious manifesto of the United Nations.

Shady schemes never really sound badly or appear harmful at the outset. On the contrary, they are filled with common analogies and lofty ideology coated with lots of love and understanding towards all. A study of the finer points normally divulges a lot about the architects and this case is no exception.

The URI, in its number one principle, states it is not a religion, but its dogmas and true leader, the Antichrist, have stated otherwise. The first ten principles seem to be rather unpretentious.

1. The URI is a bridge-building organization, not a religion.

2. We respect the sacred wisdom of each religion, spiritual expression and indigenous tradition.

3. We respect the differences among religions, spiritual expressions and indigenous traditions.

4. We encourage our members to deepen their roots in their own tradition.

5. We listen and speak with respect to deepen mutual understanding and trust.

6. We give and receive hospitality.

7. We seek and welcome the gift of diversity and model practices that do not discriminate.

8. We practice equitable participation of women and men in all aspects of the URI.

9. We practice healing and reconciliation to resolve conflict without resorting to violence.

10. We act from sound ecological practices to protect and preserve the Earth for both present and future generations.

11. We seek and offer cooperation with other interfaith efforts.

12. We welcome as members all individuals, organizations and associations who subscribe to the Preamble, Purpose and Principles.

When you reach the thirteenth principle, the tone changes.

13. We have the authority to make decisions at the most local level that includes all the relevant and affected parties.

Who gave this authority to them or did they just seize it?

14. We have the right to organize in any manner at any scale, in any area, and around any issue or activity that is relevant to and consistent with the Preamble, Purpose and Principles.

It appears that local laws are meaningless to the URI. This framework resembles the foundation upon which the National Police Force is built. First, local laws are ignored, and the National Police take over local law enforcement, eventually the National Police Force answers directly to the UN. All of this is thanks to Bill Clinton who signed away our sovereignty.

The rest of the principles are listed below.

15. Our deliberations and decisions shall be made at every level by bodies and methods that fairly represent the diversity of affected interests and are not dominated by any.

16. We (each part of the URI) shall relinquish only such autonomy and resources as are essential to the pursuit of the Preamble, Purpose and Principles.

17. We have the responsibility to develop financial and other resources to meet the needs of our part, and to share financial and other resources to help meet the needs of other parts.

18. We maintain the highest standards of integrity and ethical conduct, prudent use of resources, and fair and accurate disclosure of information.

19. We are committed to organizational learning and adaptation.

20. We honor the richness and diversity of all languages and the right and responsibility of participants to translate and interpret the Charter, Articles, Bylaws and related documents in accordance with the Preamble, Purpose and Principles, and the spirit of the United Religions Initiative.

21. Members of the URI shall not be coerced to participate in any ritual or be proselytized.

The membership list of the URI is quite diverse. It contains members from nearly every religion and from big businesses around the globe. Politicians and cabinet members like Colin Powell are high on the list. Why would these people need to take control of local situations?

If their purpose is purely peaceful, why are there concentration camps awaiting prisoners across the globe? Perhaps it is impossible to stop the URI, the New World Order and their chief henchmen. Each day we are seeing new inroads to the New World Order.

Gorbachev comes up in the Bible Code, along with some very interesting words. The results are on the next page.

Found In Numbers 15:35

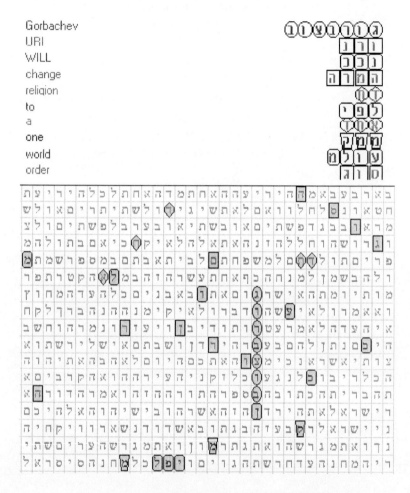

Gorbachev
URI
WILL
change
religion
to
a
one
world
order

Have you noticed the latest multilingual commercials hitting the airwaves? Everyday, our cultural and national boundaries are being chipped away making diversity appear glamorous. Boundaries, however, are not bad or the preservation of different cultures. Although the URI boasts of protecting those differences, in the end, all the lines will be blurred, forcing us all to march to the beat of one drummer, one infamous leader.

The drum will force a new cadence on us all where we will be absorbed into one religion, one law and one global leader. Those who can't keep step will be killed. It is that simple.

We are being dumbed down, failing to recognize that our liberties are being removed. In a utopian environment, perhaps the principles of the URI, if honestly designed, followed without the hidden agenda, would be marvelous to a degree. It is the failure of the URI and the UN to distinguish and to honor personal freedoms and beliefs contrary to their own dubious doctrines.

Gorbachev's World Forum believes strongly in global governance. That governance is crucial and just as pivotal is their control over the private sector, especially at local levels. Even the media has been conscripted to offer global coverage of World Forum events. The US media for some time has been under the same one world thumb, although they still maintain network identification.

Winning over the major networks is a vital aspect not only for this particular rode to Rome, but for the UN and the Antichrist who have literally captured the major sectors in the global market. With the media reporting their party line, the average person, especially those without Internet access haven't a clue about their plans.

Americans have demonstrated the proof of our complacency during the 2000 election. Some passionate pockets of Americans championed either Bush or Gore and organized behind their candidate. For the most part though, the majority seemed to express no real interest or concern. Perhaps that is because our individual comfort zones were not disrupted.

Decisions are being made for us everyday, and often, we don't hear about them for months or in some cases, years. By then, it is too late to do anything. The concentration camps were built for us without our knowledge or permission, using our dollars. Yet, they are there waiting for us.

There are many of us whose names have been placed in international databases, who will be the first to try out the beds at those new prisons. Millions more will be joining us when they refuse to take the Antichrist's Mark.

Soon, very little truth will emerge from the media and we will get our daily dose of UN acceptable "news," for those who even bother to watch.

Our youth have always been targeted and the URI and the World Forum haven't forgotten that. Both are working very hard to capture the hearts and minds of our youth by providing a special Emerging Leaders Program. They encourage "our leaders of tomorrow by having them become leaders of today."

Hitler had his youth movement and so does Gorbachev. It takes little imagination to see where the recruitment of our children will lead. No doubt, they will be integral participants, who will be in the position of reporting on non-UN concepts within the home. The UN has made it clear that children have the right to live their lives the way they want, to engage in premarital sex and to have access to abortions if necessary.

If we think mind control is out of the question, we need to look at what is already in place in some states. In California, children are encouraged to report to school officials if their parents own guns. Many women's health organizations back abortions for girls without parental knowledge or consent. Some of those groups even give classes, which instruct girls to file for emancipation from their parents and in some cases, legal fees are provided to accomplish this.

Abortion comes up in the Bible Code and the results are on the next page.

Found in Exodus 11:1

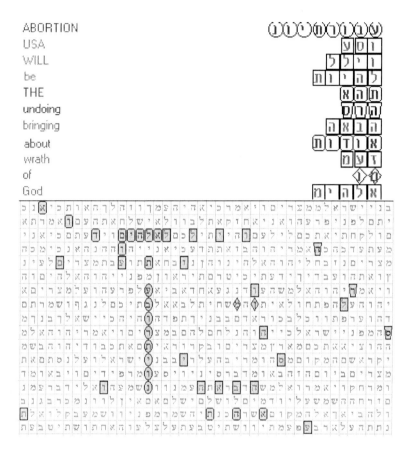

The programs may be diverse in nature and separated by thousands of miles, but they have the same architects. Those architects are calling the shots and pulling the strings. It is all connected. Everything is headed into one vortex and it is called the United Nations.

We are quickly being classified and filed under specific categories by US law enforcement, whose agencies report to the super global database.

As an example, when Y2K was making everyone nervous, the FBI had a strategic assessment done to give them an idea about possible domestic terrorism. The assessment was done in part to evaluate various threats and offer solutions to law enforcement. Project Megiddo is an eye-opening report that did not become obsolete after Y2K fizzled into a non-issue. In fact, anything apocalyptic in nature still gets the Bureau's undivided attention.

Some of the topics covered include a dissertation about when the millennium truly began, a blueprint for action in response to the Turner Diaries, Interpretations of the Bible, Apocalyptic Religious Beliefs, The New World Order Conspiracy beliefs and Gun Control Issues.

The assessment further details information on Christian Identity groups, white supremacists, militias, Black Hebrew Israelites, apocalyptic cults and the Significance of Jerusalem.

First, let's look at the name of the project: Project Megiddo. Situated in northern Israel is the hill called Megiddo where many battles have taken place. The apocalyptic term "Armageddon" means the hill of Megiddo. Armageddon is normally associated with the final battle where God and evil will meet. So, the FBI thought the Project Megiddo was "aptly named" because of some people's fears that 2000 would be the year of that last great battle. It was thought that some groups would initiate violence in order to start the countdown to Armageddon.

Part of the fear, on many people's minds, as we approached 2000, was based on whether our computers and the systems running this country and the world would shut down. That was a legitimate concern and obviously we have weathered that. However, most of the concerns for the new millennium were based on the fact the FBI felt extremist groups placed excessive significance on the new millennium. Law enforcement apparently felt the pressure resulting from that.

People who believed in apocalyptic scenarios came under intense scrutiny from law enforcement. Evidence seems to show that the scrutiny has not ceased once we passed the 2000 mark. The main dilemma for law enforcement, as stated in Project Megiddo, "the fundamental problem is that the traditional focal point for counter-terrorism analyzes –the terrorist group—is not always well defined or relevant in the current environment."

Although Project Megiddo turned up very few murmurings about explicit threats, the FBI still considers the possibility of domestic terrorism as viable. The report cited that even though major factions like the Christian Identity Movement, may not publicly call for violence, some of their fringe members might believe violence is the only way to bring about change.

Certain fringe members of these groups started to stockpile weapons, food, clothing, and to raise funds for alleged terrorist activities. The FBI feels that cult-related violence challenges law enforcement to a greater extent. Therefore, Project Megiddo recommended that individual cult leaders should come under surveillance. According to the report, it was felt that many cults believe in a fiery end and should be observed closely.

Fears of sustained terrorism to prevent the New World Order have lingered long after 2000. The Federal Government is very worried about being targeted by such cults. Although, it could conceivably be argued that Bin Laden has more harmful intentions against the government and the US than US citizens.

Supposedly, militias are connecting possible power outages as NWO devices. Apparently, this is still true. The rolling blackouts in California have a lot of people speculating as to the cause and the people behind them. When a massive power outage hit the West a few years ago, prophets said that the New World Order was experimenting with the populace to see what it would do.

With power shortages more prevalent in 2001, and the likelihood they will widen, it appears the prophets may be correct.

Whatever is going on, it hasn't stopped the FBI from scrutinizing American citizens. Throughout Project Megiddo, the NWO was brought up as a catalyst for many militia groups. Still, the report never denied the existence and ultimate implementation of the NWO. Actually, the report made the existence and future of the NWO a foregone conclusion.

For years, I have spoken out about the presence of guillotines in the United States and around the world. First reports of the influx of guillotines came in the 1980's following the Rex 84 concentration camps. A valuable government source confirmed that many more guillotines had come into the US through Denver and were being distributed throughout all the FEMA centers.

Visionaries concurred that the guillotines were here and that they would soon be put into use. There has been a worldwide trend to re-establish guillotines as the prime choice for executions. Those backing this method of extermination feel it is the most humane answer to capital punishment.

The guillotine was named for a French physician Joseph Ignace Guillotin. It was his suggestion in 1789, to use a blade designed for executions. The original guillotine was made of two upright posts connected at the top by a crossbeam. Grooves on the inside of the upright posts formed tracks for the oblique blade to fall after the rope holding it was released. A similar machine was used during the French Revolution.

The guillotine became notorious after famous people lost their heads, such as Anne Boleyn, Marie Antoinette, Charles I, of England, Adolph Eichmann and Saint Ignasius of Antioch.

Now the guillotine is making a big come back and it was updated recently. Gone is the old rope mechanism, replaced by a blade that is electrically run. Hydraulics arm the blade and speed up the entire process. Even the single person guillotine has been replaced. Guillotines can now accommodate four or more individuals at one time.

This method of execution has been championed as the most humane method of execution. However, tests have been run which indicate a person's brain still functions normally for about fifteen seconds after the head has been severed from the body. A chilling thought for any guillotine candidate. Still, it has also been proven that the hydraulic guillotines are so quick, that the process is painless.

At last estimate, over 3,000 guillotines have been imported from France. With the use of multi-person guillotines, it would be quite easy to dispose of hundreds of thousands of people who fail to comply with the New World Order, the United Nations and the Antichrist.

The word guillotine appears in the Bible Code and the results are below.

Found In Genesis 44:9

guillotine
used
to
control
people
who
fight
THE
new
world
order

112 KEATING

Guillotine

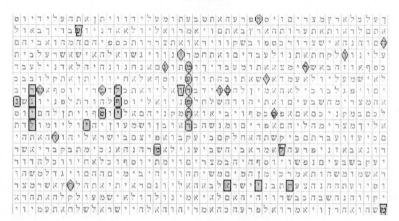

Chapter Ten

As I mentioned in the last chapter, the FBI did not deny that the New World Order exists, but does it really exist or is it a myth perpetuated by some fringe Americans? Ira Strauss, who has written a great deal about conspiracy theories said, "Conspiracy theory is doing America real harm. Long incubating underground, it has grown into the greatest enslaver of human minds since communism. It irrationalizes thinking on every issue. It kills. It turns millions of Americans against their own country. It undermines foreign policy by vilifying our government's every effort."

The Strauss essay, *"When Conspiracy Theory Replaces Thought,"* is best summed up by the subtitle of the book, "The US is threatened by Americans who believe Washington is part of a plot to enslave us in a New World Order." Does the shoe fit?

Strauss, a US coordinator of the Committee in Eastern Europe and Russia in NATO, is a front man in the concerted global effort to demonize anyone who speaks out against the NOW. People are also considered global enemies of the NOW if they discuss the NOW's connection with the Trilateral Commission, the Federal Reserve and the Council on Foreign Relations. People like Strauss try to diminish investigative reporters like Barry Chamish who have successfully linked these groups to the NOW and their designs to take over the world.

Regardless of the mounting evidence, the government, Strauss and company downplay the existence of their elite group, calling their detractors nut cases. Those nut cases, incidentally, end up on an Interpol list of "problem people," who no doubt will be the first people to be silenced.

"Once a mind is trapped in the circular logic of conspiracy theory, it rarely finds a way out on its own," Strauss said. He continues in a finger pointing statement, "crackpots infected with such 'Birchest fantasy' are capable of blowing up federal buildings."

Supposed "crackpots" are put on a watch list if they mention the Bilderbergers, Henry Kissinger, the Rockefellers, the Illuminati or the Council on Foreign Relations. Merely mentioning any of the above is considered a "Potential Warning sign," that according to its author, Dr. John J. Nutter, "an individual is active in an extremist group or planning violent or criminal activity." Nutter is a media guru who is touted as an expert on extremism. So, does Nutter intend to some investigative reporters to the Oklahoma City bombing?

There is a Leninist quality in people who have to silence their opposition. Lenin wrote, "We can and we must write in a language which sows among the masses hate, revulsion, scorn and the like, toward those who disagree with us." Had Lenin lived longer, he might have become Secretary General at the UN.

To deny the existence of the New World Order is akin to saying the Mafia doesn't exist. Until Joseph Valachi testified before Congress in 1963, and told the world about the Cosa Nostra, very few people admitted the mob actually existed. Nevertheless, the mob was an international syndicate which organized crime at its twisted best.

Maurice Malkin, the founder of the Communist Party, USA, wrote about the strange relationship of the Mafia and the Communists in his book, "*Return to My Father's House.*"

It seems the Communist Party in the US has had a standing agreement with the Mafia since 1924. Under this agreement, the Mafia agreed to do work for the Communist Party International. In this accord, the Mafia consented to murder opponents, to launder money, to counterfeit, to steal government documents and anything else Communist agents could not carry out by themselves.

Sources indicate a major change in Kremlin policy during the 1950's, which included branching out to all Mafia families around the world.

General Major Jan Sejna, from Czechoslovakia, was a defector who detailed Communist plans in the book, *Red Cocaine*, by Dr. Joseph Douglas. According to Sejna, by infiltrating organized crime, the Communists could control politicians and have open access to drugs, weapons and all the money they needed.

Communists continued their global expansion following their manifesto, Programs of the Communist International, which was unanimously accepted by the 6th Congress in Moscow in 1928.

Many top officials in the Roosevelt administration were believers in this programme and a trend of a more socialistic country began to emerge here in the United States. An abundance of Communists and communist sympathizers were appointed to sensitive government positions. We began to see more American bankers and financiers arranging loans and financial aid to the Kremlin.

Large organizations with tax-exempt status like Rockefeller, Carnegie and Ford, were instrumental in distributing vast sums of money to socialist and communist organizations. It was even discovered that the US foundations had communists on staff. One of the most publicized cases involved Soviet spy Algier Hiss, who was appointed to head the Carnegie Foundation.

In a congressional investigation in 1953, Ford Foundation president, H. Rowan Gaither told researcher Norman Dodd, that federal agencies "operated under directives issued by the White House, the substance of which was to the effect that we should make every effort to so alter life in the United States as to make possible a comfortable merger with the Soviet Union."

Many investigators were surprised to learn that orders for the communist party in the States did not come from Moscow, but rather from three wealthy American businessmen at the Waldorf Towers in New York City.

Robert Welch, founder of the John Birch Society wrote in his essay, *"The Truth in Time,"* the communist movement is only a tool of the total conspiracy. Welch was sure that the seat of power was not Moscow, but rather, here in the West.

There is more proof that the NOW was the plan of a few super wealthy individuals with monumental global plans. Those plans are solidified and moving forward quite rapidly.

We are seeing an abundant number of CFR members working for President Bush. These members have one goal in mind and that is the furthering of the NWO without regard to the populace. It doesn't matter if the US is sold out or whether they employ the Mafia or absorb communist dogma. The only thing that matters is the implementation of the NOW structure. That structure has very few bricks left before it is complete. The UN, a branch of the NOW, has been extremely successful in organizing the takeover of the World. Here in the US, we have seen President Clinton hand over millions of acres of land and rivers to the UN.

Clinton also made other moves sympathetic to the UN in his executive orders, which President Bush has failed to rescind. Landowners are being stripped of their rights and their ownership. Soon, the notion of private property will only be given to CFR members and NOW proponents. Idaho Representative Helen Chenoweth said it best about Clinton's curious give away.

"You've destroyed ethics, morals, home and God."

One of the door prizes in Clinton's land grab was, of course, the incredible coal deposit beneath the Utah preserve he created, as perhaps payola to the Lippo Group, the Indonesian group implicated in illegal fundraising for the Democrats. The Lippo Group, not surprisingly, has been developing massive coal projects in Asia. With the Utah coal out of the picture, the Asian mines will be more significant.

As we race to Rome on this expensive toll bridge, we are getting more reports of black helicopter flights all over the country. The military arm of the NWO is flexing its considerable muscle, first to intimidate and ultimately, to move in on us.

The so-called accident near Hainan, involving a US military spy plane and a Chinese fighter jet may be the latest indication that we're about to move to the next level on the NOW agenda. If the plane was set down to deliver US technology to the Chinese, or if it was just some strange war dance in the skies really doesn't matter. It is a stepping-stone to increased tensions and mounting global problems devised to sucker the US into more military involvement overseas.

That participation will make us even more vulnerable at home, leaving us open to attack and subsequent invasion. Increasing numbers of government sources agree with visionary predictions that we could see war in the US before the end of 2001. This is another signal that the final stages of NOW plans are nearing fruition.

Rolling blackouts will be another integral aspect for these plans to be fulfilled. Earthquakes and storms will continue to keep us off guard aiding the NWO movement and its schemes.

Should we have a nuclear strike or biological attack here in this country, martial law will usher in the UN. This will not be a temporary fix to restore law and order, but a permanent "solution" for America. Our glory days and more importantly, our freedoms will be gone forever.

How is this possible? About 3,000 people are controlling the world and its money in the Council on Foreign Relations. Several hundred US members are working diligently to accomplish the goal. Many are government officials, as previously mentioned. However, many members are elite people with the US media. Other members are spread throughout the banking industry, colleges, and universities and even the military.

When Congress shut down America's entry into the League of Nations, a group of British and American diplomats headed to Paris in 1919 to commiserate. Determined to destroy national sovereignty throughout the world, they decided to organize the British Royal Institute for International affairs and the Council on Foreign Relations. President Woodrow Wilson's top advisor, Edward Mandell House, was the leader of this group. He was an avowed socialist in love with Karl Marx's ideas.

House wrote a book espousing his beliefs in 1912.

In the book, *Philip Dru: Administrator*, House described the plan for drastically changing the American system by orchestrating a takeover based on "Socialism as dreamed of by Karl Marx."

Rockefeller and Carnegie funded the undertaking and soon prominent Americans were members of the CFR. In 1939, they cultivated a relationship with the US Department of State and easily became the dominant force in foreign policy. It is only necessary to look at Roosevelt's domestic and foreign programs to confirm the degree of CFR influence.

In 1974, Richard N. Gardner, a Columbia University professor, wrote a disturbing article entitled, *"The Hard Road to World Order."* This former State Department employee promoted the cause to have "and end-around national sovereignty eroding it piece by piece."

Gardner's article beautifully laid out CFR rules and guidelines clearly displaying contempt for the US Constitution. Of interest, is that this article created quite a fuss in Washington, but no members of the CFR were asked to resign their government positions. Those government employees had sworn an oath to uphold the very Constitution they sought to destroy.

We are paying for their duplicitous behavior and we have witnessed substantial erosion of our sovereignty.

The CFR was instrumental in taking over governments world wide and installing leaders who were CFR members. Robert McNamara and Dean Rusk were pivotal players in Cuba and Viet Nam, who made sure the Bay of Pigs and the Viet Nam war were utter failures.

The Council on Foreign Relations came up in the Bible Code. The results are below.

Found In Numbers 28:26

COUNCIL
foreign
relations
want
control
of
THE
temple
mount
for
anti-
christ

Council on Foreign Relations

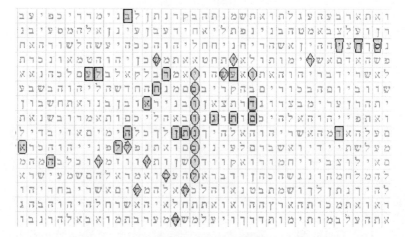

A big piece of the NWO plan came when the US gave back the Panama Canal. There is now a huge influx of Chinese military personnel utilizing the canal and migrating through Central America and Mexico, poised to invade our southern borders. Our US border patrol officers have been fired upon by Chinese soldiers dressed in Mexican army fatigues. The takeover of the US is getting closer.

Chapter Eleven

There is one spot of land in the world that is considered the most sacred place on earth. It is also the one hallowed spot that has people willing to go to war to possess it. That site is the Temple Mount on Mount Mariah in Jerusalem.

The stone or bedrock under the Dome of the Rock is called the Foundation Stone. The term Foundation Stone comes from the creation of the earth by God on the "first day." According to Jewish tradition, the bedrock was called the Foundation Stone because the whole world was founded on it. Indeed, the Temple Mount is considered the exact center of the earth.

The Arabic inscription on the western façade of the Dome of the Rock says, "The Rock of the Temple from the Garden of Eden." At the northern gate of the mosque there is another inscription, "Gate of Paradise." On the ground in front of the gate, there is a green jasper stone, which is called, "The Stone of Eden." Supposedly, the Stone of Eden covers the hole to the great abyss. Although, in 1911, the stone was removed and only a shallow hole was revealed. This sacred ground on Mount Mariah is the site where God asked Abraham to offer Isaac as a sacrifice. God led Abraham to Mount Mariah. There, Abraham built an altar and gathered wood for the fire. Isaac, Abraham's son, asked him where the lamb was for the sacrifice.

Abraham said, "My son, God will provide for Himself the lamb for the burnt offering." (Gen. 22:7,8)

Abraham raised the knife to kill Isaac as God had commanded, but at the last moment, God intervened and Isaac was spared. Even today, the site is called the Lord Will Provide or Yahweh Sireh. This event happened around 1760 in the Jewish year or around 2000 BC.

In Moses' time, God began to show Himself as a merciful God who wanted to dwell among His people and to reveal Himself to them. God told Moses that He wanted to be the Jews constant companion, to comfort them and to care for them. God told Moses to build the Tabernacle in the middle of their camp, similar to what kings and Bedouin chiefs would do. In fact, God gave Moses specific plans for the construction.

Those plans consisted of a tent approximately forty-five feet long, which was divided into two parts by a veil. The entrance room was approximately 30 feet by 15 feet and it was known as "the Holy Place." The ark of incense was located in the center of that room. That ark was about 3 feet high. Incense, aromatic resins and some charcoal were burned there two times per day. A menorah or seven-branched candlestick was on the left of this ark or altar. To the right was located the Table of Showbreads. The bread honored the twelve tribes of Israel and consequently, there were twelve loaves placed on the table in two stacks of six. The bread was placed there every Sabbath.

On the other side of the veil was the Holy of Holies, where the Ark of the Covenant rested. Located above the Ark was the Mercy Seat.

God designed the Ark, which was supposed to be made out of wood. The specifications were designed to perfectly house the Ten Commandments given to Moses on two tablets. The Ark also contained Aaron's rod, which budded, and also a pot of manna.

This chest was approximately four feet long and two and a half feet high and made of acacia wood. Gold completely covered the chest both inside and out. On the sides of the chest were rings in which poles could pass through and be used to carry the Ark.

On top of the Ark, the Mercy Seat consisted of two gold cherubim, whose job was to guard and to protect.

Once a year, on the Day of Atonement, the High Priest sprinkled the Seat with the blood of the sacrifice. Of all the holy places, this was the holiest and represented the visible throne of God. From this sacred place, God spoke to His people.

Each time the Israelites would stop during their journey, they were to build this Tabernacle. However, the ultimate goal was to build a permanent Tabernacle.

When Joshua succeeded Moses, the Jews were led into Canaan. The Tent remained in Shiloh with them until Shiloh was destroyed around 1050 BC. It was never rebuilt.

The Philistines took the Ark of the Covenant until David returned the Ark to Jerusalem. Tradition has it that David placed the Ark on top of Mount Mariah. This was to be the final location of the Ark and the Tabernacle.

King David felt awkward because his palace was made out of cedar, but the Lord dwelled in only a tent. So, he decided to design a substantial home or Temple for God.

David soon found out that he would not be the builder of the Temple. Instead, God told David that his son, Solomon, would be the one to build it. This permanent Temple was to be a constant reminder to the Jews not to worship idols.

Solomon built the Temple with the help of Hiram of Tyre and around 184,000 workers. It took seven years to build the Temple, which was made using cedar, limestone and huge amounts of silver and gold.

In 910 BC, the Temple was plundered under the direction of Pharaoh Sheshak of Egypt.

The King of Judah, Joash, rebuilt the Temple in 835 BC. Then in 720 BC, Akaz was King of Judah and he put in a Syrian altar in the Temple and dismantled Solomon's bronze vessels.

The Assyrians tried to capture Jerusalem in 716 BC, but Hezekiah, King of Jerusalem, fought them off. The Temple was then restored. In 587 BC, Nebuchadnezzar destroyed the Temple and took the sacred vessels to Babylon. He also murdered scores of people in Jerusalem and took the few remaining Jews, holding them in captivity.

Ezekiel received a vision from God, which showed him that a new Temple would be built in the age of the Messiah. This was in 573 BC. At the same time, Jeremiah prophesied that the Jews would be held captive in Babylon for seventy years.

When the Jews returned to Jerusalem at the end of those seventy years, they constructed another Temple, which was complete in 515 BC.

Alexander the Great descended on Jerusalem but was persuaded not to destroy the city. Apparently, Jewish priests showed him Scriptures that predicted his rise to power. After Alexander died, Egypt and Syria fought in the Holy Land.

Antiochus desecrated the Temple in 167 BC, but the table was later purified in 165 BC. However, the Jews did not have supervision of the Temple until the Maccabees beat the Roman Akva Fortress.

In 63 BC, Rome conquered the Holy Land. Pompey entered the Holy of Holies, but found it empty.

The Second Temple was rebuilt and enlarged. The First and Second Temples were built on the same foundation. The site had to be consecrated. Pagans could not have previously used for it for worship. Some say the location of the Holy of Holies was the exact center of the earth.

Jesus was circumcised and named in the grand courts of the refurbished Second Temple.

Twelve years later, Jesus amazed religious leaders with His knowledge of scripture. During his public life, Jesus threw out the moneychangers from the Temple. Jesus also predicted the destruction of that Second Temple.

On the 9th day of Av, in 70 AD, Roman General Titus razed the Temple. Every stone in the Temple was torn apart. Subsequent eras of Romans, Muslims and Crusaders left a great deal of doubt concerning the original location of the Temple.

The traditional site of the Temple seems to be under the Muslim Shrine, the Dome of the Rock. The majority of rabbis in Jerusalem today believe this is accurate.

A Jerusalem archaeologist, Dr. Dan Bakat, is convinced through his work and study that this is the correct site. Some disagreement with Dr. Bakat has surfaced. Dr. Asher Kaufman believes the actual Temple site may be 330 feet to the north of the Dome of the Rock.

Part of the outcropping of bedrock is under the Islamic Shrine called, "The Dome of the Tablets." Kaufman thinks that under a small canopy, which is supported by two columns, is where the original Temples lie.

Tuvin Sagiv disagrees with Kaufman's premise and believes in the Southern Conjecture. One aspect of Sagiv's Southern Conjecture is that "living water" or fresh water had to be used by Temple priests for mikvehs or ritual baths and for washing the Temple.

In studying the aqueducts, it showed that if the Temple had been built under the Dome of the Rock, the aqueduct would have been twenty meters too low. Therefore, the Temple must have been built lower, approximately twenty meters to the south.

Sagiv also used penetrating radar probes, which suggest that vaults and even rabbinical arches or kippim are south of the Dome.

No matter which conjecture is correct, Kaufman's or Sagiv's, it will be nearly impossible to know unless and until a meticulous archaeological investigation is conducted under the Temple Mount.

Currently, the Temple Mount is not under Jewish supervision, but rather under the Supreme Muslim Council. They have refused to allow any investigations or studies.

Still, the Jews are determined to rebuild the Temple. Preparations of vessels, vestments and tools used in the Temple have been underway for years. Just as determined are the Muslims who will fight anyone attempting to throw them off that contested rock on Mount Mariah.

Ariel Sharon nearly started Armageddon when he deliberately went to the Temple Mount. The violent effects of his visit are still being felt. Since his election as prime minister, Sharon has aggressively pushed for the Temple reconstruction and pushed to get the Arabs out of Israel

Yet, his diligence and desire to build the Third Temple may not be nobly or religiously motivated. Instead, he may be part of a global effort orchestrated by the CFR to rebuild the Temple.

Sharon has a big hurdle to cross and that is the Muslims who don't want to part with the Dome of the Rock or the land underneath it. Further, the Taliban and Palestinian Muslims believe that everything before the creation of Islam was meaningless. The Muslims claim that the Western wall and each stone in it belongs to Muslims and not to Jews. The Muslims believe that the Temple Mount is where Mohammed rose to heaven. The Jews, of course, believe the Temple Mount is the original site of King Solomon's Temple. Neither side is willing to compromise.

With the Muslim claim that they own not only the Dome but also the land underneath it, down to the equivalent of seven stories, there is bound to be increasing Jewish hostility and resentment.

The Jews are claiming the Muslims are excavating and destroying sacred artifacts found below the Temple Mount.

A petition was filed by a group of Israelis in the High Court to stop the Muslim excavation. The petition states that, "Rare archaeological artifacts are being cursorily destroyed by the giant scale activities of the Muslim Wakf and the Islamic movement of Israel, the aim of which is to turn the entire site into an exclusively Muslim holy place."

The petition seeks the court's favor and to tell the government to order a halt to all Wakf from work that is not approved by government officials. Meanwhile, Yassar Arafat and Ariel Sharon are polarized over this prized spot of land and likely will remain so. Most analysts concur that Sharon's visit to the Temple Mount is the cause of the latest violence in Israel and that it could quite easily escalate into full-blown war.

Peace talks at Camp David failed to produce results when neither Ehud Barak nor Arafat would agree to give up the Temple Mount. So the Muslim excavation of the Jewish holy site continues, making peace impossible.

In a surprising move against his own people, former Prime Minister Ehud Barak granted construction permits to the Wakf to continue their desecration of the Temple Mount. According to some well-placed Israeli sources, Barak either didn't know what was going on or if he did, he was a complete idiot.

All artifacts confirming the site as a Jewish holy site are being destroyed. For centuries, the Muslims have claimed Jerusalem as their most holy site and naturally, so have the Jews. Supposedly, the Muslim claim to Jerusalem is based on the Koran. However, Jerusalem is not even mentioned in the Koran, although a "Furthest Mosque" is mentioned in Sura 17:1, "Glory be unto Allah who did take his servant for a journey at night from the Sacred Mosque to the Furthest Mosque."

There doesn't seem to be any reason to believe that the Dome of the Rock is that mosque.

When Mohammed died in 632, Jerusalem was predominantly Christian. The Church that was built on the Temple Mount was the Church of Saint Mary of Justinian. It was a Byzantine church built in the Byzantine style of architecture.

Jerusalem was captured by Khalif Oman in 638. Khalif Abd built Aksa Mosque or the Dome of the Rock, in 691-692. The final reconstructed mosque on the Temple Mount wasn't finished until 80 years after Mohammed died, around 711. Therefore, it could not have been the mosque in Mohammed's mind when he put together the Koran. Most scholars firmly believe the Mosque at Mecca was the mosque Mohammed had in mind. In fact, Mohammed had a strict law about not facing Jerusalem in prayer.

Currently, Israel wants to hand over the Temple Mount to the UN in an effort to bring peace with the Palestinians. The US is behind this move as well as Egypt, France and UN Secretary General, Kofi Annan. This international control of Jerusalem and the Temple Mount is critical in the final stages of the New World Order's plans, placing the Antichrist on the throne in the soon-to-be-built Third Temple.

Jewish citizens who were protesting Arabs at the Lions Gate in Jerusalem attacked the Arab control of the Mount and recently, many Jews. Israeli citizens have long been appalled at the Israeli government's refusal to curb the Muslim excavation. Sooner or later, a religious war of great magnitude will break out. This will provide for the entrance of the Antichrist as he brings peace, however temporary, to the Middle East.

It has been noted that the Israeli government has protected shrines of other religions, but for some strange reason, they are not protecting a most sacred shrine to Judaism.

Something, someone or perhaps a group of people with a vested interest in the Temple Mount are more than likely controlling the main officials within the Israeli government.

With Christians pushing for Jerusalem to be the new capitol, things should get very interesting in the near future.

Mount Mariah came up in the Bible Code and the results are below.

Found in Leviticus 8:25

Mount Mariah	
temple	
mount	
PLO	
CFR	
take	
control	
DIG	
for	
fake	
document	
to	
RUIN	
Rome	

Chapter Twelve

The Knights of Templar have been admired and despised. Depending on individual perspective, they are either heroes or heretics. These heroes and/or heretics have their eyes on the Temple mount and more importantly, on the treasures that lie beneath it. The Knights history has been dissected by many scholars over the years and, at the least, modified by the Knights Templar public relations machine.

According to the Knights Templar organization, "The Knights Templar is a Christian oriented fraternal organization that was founded in the 11th Century...all Knights Templar are members of the world's oldest fraternal organization known as 'The Ancient Free and Accepted Masons!'" That seems to be a major contradiction.

So, let's look at the Knights Templar from a more objective historical vantage point. Shortly after the Crusades, the knights returned home. However, keeping Jerusalem free from Mohammedan influence proved to be an ongoing problem.

In 1118, a Knight of Champlain, Hagues De Payens, and eight fellow knights decided to make a perpetual vow to defend the Christian kingdom. This vow took place during the reign of King Baldwin II who allowed these knights to live in a section of his palace, which was attached to the Temple. Their original title was "pauvres chevaliers du Temple" or Poor Knights of the Temple.

At first, being poor summed up the Knights existence living only on alms. Their early duties were to escort travelers from Jerusalem to Jordan.

De Payens went west to find recruits for the order and to seek the Church's approbation. He attended the Council of Troyes in 1128 and assisted St. Benedict. In addition to the crusaders vow of poverty, the also took perpetual vows of chastity and obedience. They chose a white habit and placed over it a red cross.

In spite of the severity of their lifestyle, young men flocked to the order in droves. There were four ranks within the Knights Templar:

Knights—well-equipped, heavy cavalry.
Sergeants—formed light cavalry.
Farmers—in charge of temporal needs.
The Chaplains—vested in sacramental orders and   could handle all spiritual needs.

Historical accounts attribute the Knights success and large numbers to their religious fervor and to their militaristic ability.

The popes looked out for the Knights and had them under papal jurisdiction, meaning they were exempt from any other jurisdiction. The Knight's property was exempt from taxation. This was not popular with the clergy in the Holy Land who felt the Knights had far too many advantages. In 1156, the clergy raised strong objections to the Knights Templar, but Rome dismissed their complaints, further widening the gap between them.

Jacques de Vitry described the Knights in his time, "in turn lions of war and lambs at the hearth; rough knights on the battlefield, pious monks in the chapel; formidable to the enemies of Christ, gentleness itself towards His friends.

Surprisingly, this brave army was never very large. At its height, they numbered only 400.

In 1291, the Saracens cast the crusading Knights out of the Holy Land. The Templars returned to Europe and brought back some of their beliefs in Kabbalism and quickly lost favor with Rome. Pope Clement V and King Philippe IV, of France, abolished the order.

The Knights Templar Grand Master, Jacques de Molay, was executed in 1314 and the rest of the Templars were either executed with him or left Europe to avoid death. Robert the Bruce of Scotland made a vow to reclaim the Holy Land from the Saracens. He died before that was accomplished. Bruce willed that his heart be buried in the Church of the Holy Sepulcher in Jerusalem. This desire was never fulfilled and his heart was returned to Scotland and buried in Melrose Abbey.

Fellow Knights and Masons worked to achieve Bruce's goal of once again taking over Jerusalem, and specifically, the Temple Mount. Many of the Scottish Rite Masons and Knights Templar believe they are the Merovingian dynasty, or the royal bloodlines of Jesus and consequently, the rightful heirs to Jerusalem. Much of the Templar's beliefs stem from the erroneous notion that Jesus had siblings and that Mary Magdelene had given birth to Jesus' child and then took him to Scotland. These are also the core beliefs of Gnostics.

Worse accusations arose about the Templar's secret ceremonies that discussed their worship of Baphomet, an idol who is said to sometimes have the head of a goat or cat. Brother Jean Taillefer, of Gevay, in 1397 gave testimony about the actual worship practices of Knights Templar.

Taillefer was received into the order and said that during his initiation, "an idol representing a human face was placed on an altar before him." He further described the head as being reddish in color.

Some scholars believe that the head, which was bearded and discolored, represented the head of John the Baptist, who the Gnostics believe was the true Messiah. Gnostics also believe that divinity lies within each person.

Another brother who went through the inquisition regarding the Knights Templar and the mysterious head, thought it resembled the head of a demon, which struck terror in him. He was afraid to look at it.

Yet, there are those who still contend that the Knights Templar are noble and good people. However, a detour from Christian doctrine took place when the Knights veered from their vows, especially those of poverty and idolized the power of gold. Further, their adopting Masonic beliefs, coupled with their Kabbalistic and occultist tendencies, led the Knights Templar down a murky path.

That path hasn't hindered their popularity or their goals to sit on the throne in Jerusalem. In fact, they are behind the excavation going on under the Temple and seem to be involved with murderous plots.

The Knights Templar believe that the first bishop of Jerusalem was Jesus' brother James, but that is heretical since Jesus had no siblings. The Knights Templar also claims that seven other siblings, five brothers and two sisters helped James. After Jerusalem was sacked, James and his family escaped to France. After many decades, supposedly this family of the Davidic line was in every royal house in Europe and had achieved enormous wealth and power. This line of alleged descendants of Jesus called themselves Rex Deus.

It was thought that the Knights uncovered records under the Temple Mount, which indicated that the Vatican was not practicing Christianity the way it was supposed to as Christ had intended. The scrolls which detail this supposed error have been hidden and that if they were released, Rome's legacy would be jeopardized.

There is even a debate fueled by the Knights Templar that the Shroud of Turin does not depict Jesus, but rather

Jacques de Molay, who was burned at the stake, but only after being crucified.

The alleged notorious scrolls were purportedly taken to Rosslyn near Edinburgh. They were housed in a chapel built by William Sinclair. The chapel was built as a duplicate to the Herodian Temple, complete with its own Western Wall.

Since the Templars were banned, they hid their existence and kept their organization by forming the Freemasons, which spread quickly throughout Europe. The Vatican was very upset with its growth and remained at odds with the Knights Templar.

Now there seems to be an even bigger battle brewing between the Vatican and the Knights Templar over the Temple Mount. According to some sources like Barry Chamish, the Israeli leadership seems to agree with the Vatican that Israel should not be part of the Temple Mount.

However, the PLO has a say in the status of the Mount. In 2000, they began digging under the Temple Mount. Substantial mounds of dirt were dumped along with ancient artifacts from the Second Temple.

In a report published by Chamish, the Israeli government's television outlet, Channel 1, aired a video that was secretly taped under the Shrine of Omar, which was purposefully built over the Holy of Holies. The video showed that a new tunnel had been built and was headed for the heart of Solomon's and Herod's Temple.

Chamish thinks there is more to the digging by the PLO than just artifacts. He thinks they must be looking for more scrolls. Those scrolls, if found, will be used as blackmail against the Vatican, according to Chamish. It is my belief that scrolls will indeed be found and that will be the beginning of the official dismantling of the Catholic Church and the beginning of the abomination of desolation. However, I believe the scrolls are not authentic.

With the Knights Templar calling on the UN to take control of the Temple Mount, we know that effort, if successful, will cause much more harm.

It is my opinion that the tensions surrounding the Mount will continue to rise causing various factions to reach the point of war, perhaps even nuclear war. Those scrolls that allegedly will debunk the Vatican are just the first steps that the Antichrist will use to build his temple over the Holy of Holies, thus fulfilling prophecy.

The Freemasons have dedicated themselves to this goal and we know they will ultimately be successful. If Barry Chamish is correct, the Knights Templar had a lot to do with the Rabin assassination as one plank in the platform to elect a Knight as the King of Jerusalem. Apparently, the Council on Foreign Relations joins the Knights in this desire and that has further complicated the situation.

Knights Templar came up in the Bible Code. The results are below.

Found In Numbers 22:6

Templar
knight
mason
temple
mount
secret
society
NWO

Knights Templar

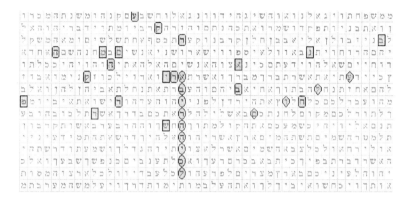

Chapter Thirteen

Without a doubt, Father Malachi Martin had to die before one of the worst frauds in history could be perpetrated. It would not have been possible for some people connected with the bogus Third Secret of Fatima to spread such outright disinformation. I believe Father Martin would have shot down the June 2000 alleged secret as the fiction that it is. Father Martin unfortunately had to die. Is it any wonder that he said on his deathbed that he had been pushed? The Bible Code relating to Father Martin seems to back up his statement.

Found in Genesis 22:11

MARTIN
Malachi
priest
knew
THE
secret
Rome
underworld
HAD
him
murdered
to
stop
talking

Fr. Malachi Martin

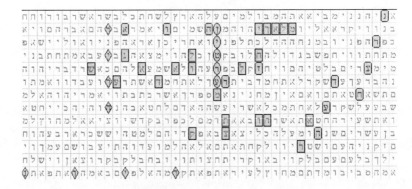

Then we are left with a lie that we are supposed to swallow. This fraudulent document released by the Vatican has divided Catholics and non-Catholics. The people who fell for the supposed Third Secret are relieved that the frightening days in our history are over for good. While those of us who know the truth realize we are in the eye of a deadly storm.

Let's look at what we know to be the truth about the original Third Secret of Fatima and compare it to the forgery.

The actual Third Secret is on one piece of paper, while the recently released secret is two pages long. The original Third Secret contained approximately 23 lines. The line count in the alleged secret is some 62 lines.

We know that the very first line in the original secret is as follows: "In Portugal, the dogma of the faith will always be preserved..." The people who had read the actual secret have known this fact. In the alleged secret, it is missing entirely.

The actual secret mentions a date, 1972, whereas the alleged secret does not. For more information on prophecies concerning 1972, please consult *The Final Warning*.

Further, handwriting experts have verified that Rome's latest attempt to deceive the world is a complete forgery.

Sister Lucy verifies this information for us. She wrote a letter to her bishop on January 9, 1944 in which she states, "I have written what you asked me. God willed to try me a little, but finally this was indeed His will: [the text] is sealed in an envelope and it is on a piece of notepaper..." Cardinal Ottavani concurs with Sister Lucy because he read the secret.

In 1955, Cardinal Ottavani interrogated Sister Lucy and then requested that the secret be brought to Rome. Before the secret was taken to Rome, Bishop Venancio, Bishop de Silva's auxiliary, held the envelope up to the light. The bishop could easily see the 23 lines in Sister Lucy's handwriting.

Venancio saw that the actual secret was written on ordinary paper. The margins on the paper were approximately ¾ centimeter on both sides.

Father Joaquin Alonso, the official archivist of Fatima, wrote at great length about the very first line in the actual secret. He wrote that the first sentence clearly indicates that the faith will be in critical condition except for Portugal. He surmised that before the Triumph of the Immaculate Heart of Mary, awful events, the topics of the Third Secret, had to occur.

Due to the lack of this subject being covered in the alleged secret, we know it is false. Pope Paul VI had read the Third Secret and seemed to discuss its contents in a speech he made April 25, 1968:

> *"Because, you know, the Church is now going through a spiritual moment of its history, which is not serene, especially in some countries...It is thus, we said, not only by reason of the practical apostasy which is so widespread, but also and especially by reason of the uneasiness which troubles certain sectors of the Catholic world and affects the sensibility of those who have responsibilities in the Church..."*

From 1968-1972, Pope Paul VI continued to speak out about a church crisis, a church that was "self-destructing" and stated on June 29th 1972, "From some fissure the smoke of Satan entered into the temple of God." Father Malachi Martin said that Satan had physically entered the Church.

In 1977, Sister Lucy met with Cardinal Albino Luciani, who would become Pope John Paul I. He came to Portugal to celebrate Mass at Sister Lucy's convent. Luciani spoke with Sister Lucy for over two hours and Sister Lucy revealed the Third Secret to him. When he emerged from the meeting, witnesses said he was visibly shaken. Luciani said, "The Secret is terrible."

Others have asked Sister Lucy about the contents of the Third Secret and her response was always, "It's in the Gospel and in the Apocalypse, read them!" When John Paul II was at Fatima, he said, "The successor of Peter prepares himself here also as a witness to the immensity of human suffering, a witness to the almost apocalyptic menaces looming over the nations and mankind as a whole."

The alleged secret is on the next page.

J. M. J.

A terceira parte do segredo
revelado a 13 de julho de 1917
na Cova da Iria — Fátima.

Escrevo em acto de obediên-
cia a vós Deus meu, que mo
mandais por meio de sua
Exc.ia Rev.ma o Senhor Bispo
de Leiria e da Tua e Minha
Santíssima Mãe.

Depois das duas partes
que já expus, vimos ao lado
esquerdo de Nossa Senhora

um pouco mais alto um
anjo com uma espada de
fogo em a mão esquerda; ao
scintilar, despedia chamas que
parecia iam incendiar o
mundo; mas apagavam se
com o contacto do brilho que
da mão direita expedia Nossa
Senhora ao seu encontro: O
anjo apontando com a mão
direita para a terra, com voz
forte disse: Penitência, Penitência, Penitência! E vimos
n'uma luz immensa que é
Deus: "algo semelhante a como
se vêm as pessoas n'um espelho

quando lhe passam por diante"
um Bispo vestido de Branco
" tivemos o pressentimento de
que era o Santo Padre". Varios
outros Bispos, Sacerdotes, religio
sos e religiosas subir uma
escabrosa Montanha, no cimo
da qual estava uma grande
cruz de troncos toscos como se
fôra de sobreiro com a casca;
o Santo Padre, antes de chegar
ai, atravessou uma grande
cidade meia em ruinas e meio
tremulo com andar vacilante,
acabrunhado de dôr e pena,
ia orando pelas almas dos cada

veres que encontrava pelo
caminho; e chegado ao sino do
monte, prostrado de joelhos
aos pés da grande Cruz foi morto
por um grupo de soldados que
lhe dispararam varios tiros e
setas, e assim mesmo foram
morrendo nos três outros os
Bispos sacerdotes, religiosos e
religiosas e varias pessoas secula-
res, cavalheiros e senhoras de varias
classes e posições sob os dois bra-
ços da cruz estavam dois anjos
cada um com um regador
de cristal em a mão, N'estes reco-
lhiam o sangue dos Martires e com
ele regavam às almas que se approxi-
mavam de Deus. Jury-3-1-1944

The translation of the Vatican's released secret is:

J.M.J.

The third part of the secret revealed at the Cova da Iria-Fatima, on 13 July 1917.

I write in obedience to you, my God, who command me to do so through his Excellency the Bishop of Leiria and through your Most Holy Mother and mine. After the two parts which I have already explained, at the left of Our Lady and a little above, we saw an Angel with a flaming sword in his left hand; flashing, it gave out flames that looked as though they would set the world on fire; but they died out in contact with the splendour that Our Lady radiated towards him from her right hand: pointing to the earth with his right hand, the Angel cried out in a loud voice: 'Penance, Penance, Penance!'. And we saw in an immense light that is God: 'something similar to how people appear in a mirror when they pass in front of it' a Bishop dressed in White 'we had the impression that it was the Holy Father'. Other Bishops, Priests, men and women Religious going up a steep mountain, at the top of which there was a big Cross of rough-hewn trunks as of a cork-tree with the bark; before reaching there the Holy Father passed through a big city half in ruins and half trembling with halting step, afflicted with pain and sorrow, he prayed for the souls of the corpses he met on his way; having reached the top of the mountain, on his knees at the foot of the big Cross he was killed by a group of soldiers who fired bullets and arrows at him, and in the same way there died one after another the other Bishops,

Priests, men and women Religious, and various lay
people of different ranks and positions. Beneath the
two arms of the Cross there were two Angels each
with a crystal aspersorium in his hand, in which they
gathered up the blood of the Martyrs and with it
sprinkled the souls that were making their way to
God. Tuy-3-1-1944.

Gary Wohlsheid of TLDM, called in Speckin Forensic
Labs to analyze the alleged Third Secret and Sister Lucy's
handwriting. Speckin found handwriting discrepancies
between the alleged Third Secret and the actual handwritten
letters by Sister Lucy. You might recall that Speckin Forensic
Labs was used in the Jon Benet Ramsey case and is known
for their reliability. The report is on the following page.

Speckin Forensic Laboratories
2105 University Park Drive, Suite A
Okemos, Michigan 48864
517-349-3528 • Fax 517-349-5538

Leonard A. Speckin
FORENSIC DOCUMENT ANALYST / CRIME SCENE SPECIALIST

Richard L. Brunelle
RETIRED INK DATING CONSULTANT

Robert D. Kullman
FORENSIC DOCUMENT ANALYST

Michael J. Sinke
LATENT PRINT SPECIALIST / FORENSIC DOCUMENT ANALYST

Roger J. Bolhouse
FORENSIC CHEMIST / TRACE EVIDENCE ANALYST

Erich J. Speckin
FORENSIC DOCUMENT ANALYST / INK DATING SPECIALIST

Thomas K. Heard, Ph.D
DNA ANALYST

Paul B. Albee, MS
COMPUTER RECOVERY SPECIALIST

Ted R. Lewis
AUDIO & VISUAL TAPE ANALYST

July 11, 2000

Mr. Gary Wohlseheid
These Last Days Ministries
P. O. Box 40
Lowell, MI 49331-0040

Dear Mr. Wohlseheid;

The following items were retrieved from Website bayside.org/news/lucy-writing.htm for examination.

QUESTIONED DOCUMENT:

    1 – Alleged text of the "Third Secret", website pages 6 through 10.

PURPORTED KNOWN WRITINGS BY SISTER LUCY:

- Letter of December 17, 1927.
- Letter of May 29, 1930.
- Letter of November 17, 1935.
- Letter of April 13, 1980.
- Letter of July 13, 1989.

EXAMINATION TASK:

My examination task is to determine if the "Third Secret" writing and the purported known writings by Sister Lucy were written by the same person.

NOTE:

The following examination results are based on the examination of documents retrieved from an Internet website. Because of the poor quality of the above listed documents, my examination is extremely limited. The detail necessary to reach a conclusive handwriting opinion is not available in reproduced documents; especially those reproduced via the Internet.

My examination is limited to overall letter formations, proportions, spacing and the format of the writing.

EXAMINATION RESULTS:

The purported known writings by Sister Lucy, covering over 50 years in time, contain numerous relatively consistent and repetitive handwriting habits, which indicates the known writings are all of the same person.

Mr. Wohlscheid
7-11-00
Page 2

EXAMINATION RESULTS Continued:

When I attempt to integrate the repetitive handwriting habits in the purported known writings by Sister
Lucy, spanning from 1927 to 1989, with the repetitive handwriting habits found in the Questioned
Document "Third Secret", I find significant formative and proportional differences between many of the
letters and letter combinations.

Many of these differences are visibly noticeable in the capital letters, such as the B, P & S; however,
because of the quality of the copies, are less detectable in the lower case letters. The more definitive
differences in the lower case letters is discoverable in the extensions below and above the base of the
writings; such as the extension of the "g" and the hump of the "h" below the base and the "t" and "l" above
the base of the writing.

I also find format differences between the margin and indentations of the purported known writings by
Sister Lucy and the Questioned Document "Third Secret".

The criteria for the identification of handwriting is that the cumulative range of variation exhibited in the
questioned writing and in the known writing contains substantial significant similarities with no
fundamental or significant differences.

Since I find a number of significant differences between the writing in the Questioned Document "Third
Secret" and the purported known writings by Sister Lucy, it is my opinion, based on the documents
examined, that the Questioned Document "Third Secret" can not be identified with the purported known
writings by Sister Lucy.

Further, it is my opinion that the number of differences noted in my comparison indicates that it is unlikely
the Questioned Document "Third Secret" was written by the same person who authored the purported
known writings by Sister Lucy.

To render a more definitive opinion it would be necessary to examine either the original documents or one
to one photographs that accurately reproduce the original documents.

Very Truly Yours,

Robert D. Kullman
Forensic Document Analyst

Speckin Forensic Laboratories
2105 University Park Drive, Suite A
Okemos, Michigan 48864
517-349-3528 • Fax 517-349-5538

Leonard A. Speckin	Michael J. Sinke	Thomas K. Huard, PhD
FORENSIC DOCUMENT ANALYST/CRIME SCENE SPECIALIST	LATENT PRINT SPECIALIST/FORENSIC DOCUMENT ANALYST	DNA ANALYST
Richard L. Brunelle	Roger J. Bolhouse	Paul B. Alter, MS
RETIRED INK DATING CONSULTANT	FORENSIC CHEMIST/TRACE EVIDENCE ANALYST	COMPUTER RECOVERY SPECIALIST
Robert D. Kullman	Erich J. Speckin	Ted R. Lewis
FORENSIC DOCUMENT ANALYST	FORENSIC DOCUMENT ANALYST/INK DATING SPECIALIST	AUDIO & VISUAL TAPE ANALYST

July 11, 2000

Mr. Gary Wohlscheid
These Last Days Ministries
P. O. Box 40
Lowell, MI 49331-0040

Dear Mr. Wohlscheid:

This is a summary of my educational background and professional qualifications.

I enlisted in the Michigan State Police in 1966 as a trooper and served in this capacity at posts in Flint and Reed City. In February of 1972 I was transferred into the Crime Laboratory to begin a three year residency training program in the questioned document section. This involves the examination of handwriting, typewriting, printing, ink, paper, photocopy machines and dating of documents. Typical cases involve the authenticating of signatures in wills, personal guaranties, contracts and identifying the author of harassing handwritten or typewritten letters. The alteration of business and medical records most often take the form of exculpatory additions made at a time subsequent to the original entries. The dating of these additions can be proved through modern forensic document examinations. The equipment used in this field ranges from simply magnifying glasses to infra red scanning instruments and E.S.D.A.

During and after my three-year residency I did additional study in forensic document analysis at Georgetown University, the U.S. Secret Service laboratory, the Federal Bureau of Investigation laboratory and Western Michigan University School of Paper Technology. I have testified as an expert witness in district courts, municipal courts, probate courts, circuit courts and federal courts, in excess of 150 times. Upon completion of my training I was promoted to Detective Sergeant and worked full time in the crime laboratory system as a forensic document analyst for nearly fourteen years until December of 1988. Since leaving the laboratory in 1988 I have continued to work as a private consultant in civil and criminal cases. In June 1998 I contracted with Mr. Leonard Speckin as a full time document analyst.

Very truly yours,

Robert D. Kuhlman
Forensic Document Analyst

The following is an example of Lucy's handwriting compared to the writing on the Vatican's secret. The sample on the left was written by Lucy on November 17, 1935. The sample on the right is from the Vatican's release.

In the next sample, we can see the difference in how Lucy wrote the word "Tuy." The example on the left is from a letter Lucy wrote on May 29, 1930. The example below it is from the Vatican's release. The "T" is clearly very different.

There has also been a lot of discussion about the Pope and the consecration of Russia to the Virgin Mary. The debate has been whether or not the consecration had ever taken place.

After a five year silence, Sister Lucy allegedly addressed the consecration issue and this time, she supposedly used a word processor, even though her sister, Caroline, said she didn't know how to type. According to sources, she made references to an alleged consecration of Russia by Pope Paul VI, but that was totally false.

For over sixty years, Sister Lucy has written about the consecration of Russia. Yet, computer generated letters from 1989-1990 contradict those previous letters.

A Fatima expert, Brother Michael of the Holy Trinity was asked about a letter Sister Lucy allegedly wrote, (computer generated) to Maria Betlem, Brother Michael said, "In this letter, it is uniquely a question of consecrating the world and never Russia. But at Fatima and then at Tuy, Our Lady never asked for the consecration of the world, but for that of Russia alone. This could refer to Pope Paul VI's statements on May 13, 1967. There is no mention of the consecration of Russia ever to have been made, namely that done by Pius XII in his apostolic letter Sacro Virgente Anno of July 7, 1952. The author therefore proves his ignorance of the Fatima question, and so the letter cannot be by Sister Lucia."

In May 1989, Cardinal Law of Boston visited Sister Lucy. She specifically told the Cardinal that the consecration of Russia still had not been made.

There was more evidence that Sister Lucy's handwriting had been forged again. This time, it was a signature attached to a computer-generated letter dated November 8, 1989. A Canadian forensic specialist declared the signature a forgery.

Fatima came up in the Bible Code and the results are on the next page.

Found In Exodus 35:15

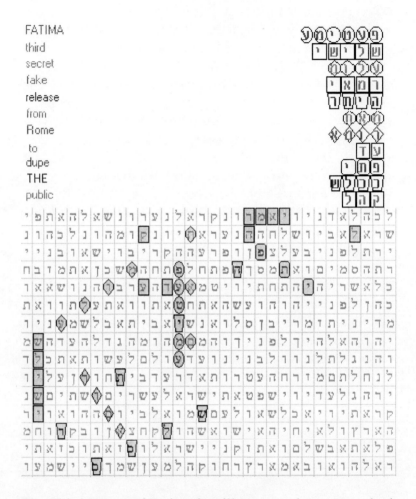

The Third Secret of Fatima is still a secret, but we can look to other apparition sites and the messages given to the visionaries, which contain the contents of the Third Secret.

The Blessed Mother appeared to a visionary in Akita, Japan. Her name is Sister Agnes Katsuko Sasagawa, and the three messages she was given have been declared by her bishop, Reverend Ito, "The message of Akita is the message of Fatima."

*"My daughter, my novice, you have obeyed
Me well in abandoning all to follow Me. Is the
infirmity of your ears painful? Your deafness
will be healed, be sure. Be patient. It is the
last trial. Does the wound of your hand cause
you to suffer? Pray in reparation for the sins
of men. Each person in this community is my
irreplaceable daughter. Do you say well the
prayer of the Handmaids of the Eucharist?
Then, let us pray it together:*

*"Most Sacred Heart of Jesus, truly present in
the Holy Eucharist, I consecrate my body and
soul to be entirely one with Your Heart being
sacrificed at every instant on all the altars of
the world and giving praise to the Father,
pleading for the coming of His Kingdom."*

*"Please receive this humble offering of myself.
Use me as You will for the glory of the Father
and the salvation of souls."*

*"Most Holy Mother of God. Never let me be
separated from your Divine Son. Please
defend and protect me as Your special child.
Amen."*

*" Pray very much for the Pope, the bishops
and the priests." July 6, 1973.*

*"My daughter, my novice, do you love the
Lord? If you love the Lord listen to what I
have to say to you."*

*"It is very important. You will convey it to
your superior."*

*"Many men in this world afflict the Lord. I
desire souls to console Him to soften the anger
of the Heavenly Father. I wish, with my Son,
for souls who will repair by their suffering and
their poverty for the sinners and ingrates."*

*"In order that the world might know His
anger, the Heavenly Father is preparing to
inflict a great chastisement on all mankind.
With my Son, I have intervened so many times
to appease the wrath of the Father. I have
prevented the coming of calamities by offering
Him the sufferings of the Son on the Cross,
His Precious Blood, and beloved souls who
console Him and form a cohort of victim
souls. Prayer, penance and courageous
sacrifices can soften the Father's anger. I
desire this also from your community, that it
love poverty, that it sanctify itself and pray in
reparation for the ingratitude and outrages of
so many men. Recite the prayer of the
Handmaids of the Eucharist with awareness of
its meaning: put it into practice: offer
(whatever God may send) in reparation for
sins. Let each one endeavor, according to
capacity and position, to offer herself entirely
to the Lord."*

*"Even in a secular institute prayer is
necessary. Already souls who wish to pray are
on the way to being gathered. Without
attaching too much attention to the form, be
faithful and fervent in prayer to console the
Master." August 3, 1973*

*". . . if men do not repent and better
themselves, the Father will inflict a terrible
punishment on all humanity. It will be a
punishment greater than the deluge, such as
one will never have seen before. Fire will fall
from the sky and will wipe out a great part of
humanity, the good as well as the bad, sparing
neither priests nor faithful. The survivors will
find themselves so desolate that they will envy
the dead. The only arms which will remain for
you will be the Rosary and the Sign left by my
Son. Each day recite the prayers of the
Rosary. With the Rosary, pray for the Pope,
the bishops and the priests."*

*"The work of the devil will infiltrate even into
the Church in such a way that one will see
cardinals opposing cardinals, bishops against
other bishops. The priests who venerate me
will be scorned and opposed by their
confreres (other priests). Churches and altars
will be sacked. The Church will be full of
those who accept compromises and the demon
will press many priests and consecrated souls
to leave the service of the Lord."*

*"The demon will be especially implacable
against the souls consecrated to God. The
thought of the loss of so many souls is the
cause of my sadness. If sins increase in
number and gravity, there will be no longer
pardon for them."*

". . . Pray very much the prayers of the Rosary.
I alone am able still to save you from the calamities
which approach. Those who place their confidence
in me will be saved." October 13, 1973

Chapter Fourteen

The one thing that has sparked the most questions, the most email and the most letters, has been on the topic of the Antichrist. I will provide an update as to his activities, his plans and his timetable.

He has appeared in thousands of people's dreams. Often, the dreams are initially filled with love and light, but normally they turn into terrifying experiences. The Antichrist has appeared in many forms, wearing distinctly different clothes from one appearance to the next. In some dreams, he tries to appear Christlike. However, the people who have seen the Antichrist appear in their dreams in flowing white robes and long hair, usually see something quite menacing in his eyes. There also seems to be an underlying theme in the dreams.

For whatever reason, be it a recognition of the man as what he is or a person's defense mechanism, most people feel the need to run away from him. Some people find it impossible to escape his grip or his hypnotic stare. Often, the only way people escape this nightmare is to call on Jesus. Invariably after invoking His name, the person will wake up.

Some people have felt compelled to visit the Antichrist's website in spite of my warnings. The majority of people who visit his site suffer major repercussions. These can range from not getting his picture out of their minds, to serious anomalous activity in their homes.

Late night visits from the Antichrist have been particularly threatening to people. Apparently, you don't have to write about him in order to garner a visit. Now, you barely have to think of him and he appears. One woman who wrote me recently didn't even have him on her mind and got quite a surprise.

She was looking at the sunset saying her prayers and focused on God. When she looked out another window of her house there was a man standing at the window looking at her. Feeling as if she was in mortal danger, the woman called on Jesus and Mary, St. Michael the Archangel and all the angels and saints for their help. Her fervent prayers were heard and the man disappeared…into thin air. After she was sure he was gone, she went outside to see his footprints in the snow, but he didn't leave any tracks. This lady felt very blessed that the dark encounter went no further and was thankful she had crucifixes on her doors and windows.

I have noticed in the year since I disclosed his name that his presence is more prevalent. People who didn't know who he is are having experiences involving him.

His supporters are running more commercials on radio and television. He has recently done local television talk shows, proving he is not a figment of his backer's imagination. The Antichrist also has many spokespeople, doing popular radio shows, laying down the foundation for his worldwide debut.

I mentioned in an article for *The Messenger,* that a statue is being built in his honor and it even bears his name. This statue will be over 500 feet tall and will house a Buddhist temple inside. The statue is being constructed in India in a town called Bogadaya, a supposed place of enlightenment. Could it be the statue of the Beast we will be commanded to worship? The British engineers from Casting Development Centre, who are leading the construction of the Temple are hoping to complete the statue by 2004. Funding for the multi-million dollar statue is pouring in from the Antichrist's organization as well as the UN.

The movement behind this man, Theosophy, has helped pave the way from the Antichrist by sculpting a new religion, which was designed to enlighten people, by first confusing them and then to ensnare them. Theosophy means Divine Knowledge and comes from the Greek. The term attained notoriety at the hands of Helena Petrovna Blavatsky.

According to Theosophists, theosophy reveals fundamental truths of all philosophers and is based primarily on Eastern philosophy.

Incorporating scientific principles and investigative techniques, theosophists try to uncover all truths. Supposedly, by revealing every conceivable fact uncovered during their investigations, an enormous library developed, eventually forming "universal doctrines" which belie Divinity in the final analysis, raising man to a "divine level." These doctrines have been guarded by people who dedicated their entire lives to their protection. It has been thought that possession and application of these doctrines resulted in great power. Power over nature and man. These doctrines can not be absorbed all at one time, according to devout theosophists, but rather doled out in miniscule increments because of their alleged power might overwhelm the user, the generation and they ultimately would boggle history. Candidates who want to attain this dangerous knowledge practice self-denial and develop a distaste for worldly ways.

Theosophy is a strange marriage of religion, albeit fractured, and science, philosophy and a dash of ethics. It is claimed that theosophy is based on reason without asserting dogmas, which are hypocritical precepts, which can't be proven. Theosophists have grown a distorted hybrid belief, which shuns Christian beliefs, while twisting their "doctrines" to control their own initiates.

The core beliefs of theosophy were put together in the late 1800's by Madame Blavatsky. Helena Petrovna Blavatsky was born in 1831 in the Ukraine. In 1849, she married Nikifor Blavatsky, but left him within a few years. She traveled extensively through Egypt, Greece and other countries, acquiring an eclectic knowledge of "ancient truths." Arriving in London in 1851, she met her Master. His name was Mahatma Morya, an Eastern initiate. Mahatma, or M. as he was later called, had appeared to Madame Blavatsky since she was a child. The new Theosophy was developed and enhanced through his instruction. Madame Blavatsky spent a great deal of time traveling through the East. In 1868, Blavatsky and her Master traveled to India and Tibet.

The Theosophist Society was founded by Madame Blavatsky in 1875. A rise in theosophists occurred after she published her first magazine called *The Theosophist* in 1879. Madame Blavatsky returned to London and established her second magazine in 1887, called *Lucifer*. Its title page contained the quote, "to bring to light the hidden things of darkness."

One of the core beliefs of theosophy is "the product of evolution of the principle spoke of from the very first forms of life guided as it proceeded by intelligent perfected beings from other and older evolutions." (from the official report of World's Parliament of Religions, 1893.) As man "ascends" to various states, it is a basis of theosophy that people grow into gods. Theosophists believe this is every persons destiny. As men's consciousness is perfected, different planes of knowledge can be attained.

Claims are made by Theosophists that Jesus subscribed to theosophical beliefs and that Jesus was a "Master," but not the Son of God, and traveled widely through India, Tibet, Persia and Egypt. We are going to hear more about that as the Antichrist comes to power. He is now the head of theosophy, weaving his own brand of religion into the end-time tapestry.

He scoffs at the Book of Revelation, as do theosophists, who deny that Jesus will come only after the world is entangled in World War III. Instead, they push the Second Coming of the Messiah as a time of great peace.

The *Encylopedic Theosophical Glossary*, Madame Blavatsky's last uncompleted work, states that the tenth, and final avatar or "Master" of Vishnu, is, "*Kalki, the avatara who is to appear at the end of the kali yuga mounted on a white horse, inaugurating a new reign of righteousness on earth. A horse has from immemorial time been a symbol of the spiritual as well as vital energies of the inner solar orb. Hence, when the next avatara is said to come riding a white horse, the meaning is that he comes infilled with the solar light or splendor – an avatara or manifestation of a spiritual and intellectual solar energy which will carry all before it on earth.*"

The similarity to the Book of Revelation is no accident.

> *And I saw Heaven opened, and behold a white horse; and he that sat upon him was called faithful and true, and with justice doth he judge and fight.* Revelation Chapter 19:11

Nor is it an accident that many Christian Churches have begun interpreting the Book of Revelation as mere symbolism.

When can we expect the Day of Declaration, the day that the Antichrist has said he will make himself known to all on the earth? As I mentioned in *The Final Warning*, the Antichrist will come onto the scene after the Great Warning. In the meantime however, he has been very busy appearing at select gatherings across the world. In fact, in 2001, the Antichrist has appeared "peacefully" from Brazil to Japan, appearing to mostly Christian groups doing his best impression of the Savior.

His "miraculous" magnetized water has purportedly resulted in
many cures. Ministers are seen on television pushing this water
on desperate people in need of a miracle. Naturally, some
miracles occur. It remains to be seen how permanent the cures
will be.

Although there will be many Antichrists, one critical
person will emerge to rule the world. It's our choice if he will
rule our hearts and souls.

False Christ comes up in the Bible Code. The results are
presented below.

Found In Leviticus 15:13

False Christ
will
work
with
THE
U.N.
bringing
about
new
world
order

Chapter Fifteen

After researching the major players and the events they have caused, it became apparent that the old saying "all roads lead to Rome," really is true. Prophecies are filled with messages of Divine Justice for the not-so eternal city. Certainly, Rome has been the prize of communists and Masons for centuries. Rome's history has been filled with greatness, with debauchery, with all things good and with all things bad. This paradoxical city will be destroyed again, once and for all.

Several things have to happen before that nuclear blast takes place, before the red flag flies over the Vatican and the city is hurled into its final battle. The recent consistory of cardinals in Rome heard Cardinal Martini's call for Vatican III. Fortunately for the world, it was shut down this time, but we know it won't be sidetracked in the future. The Bible Code mentions Vatican III and the results are on the next page.

Found In Genesis 44:12

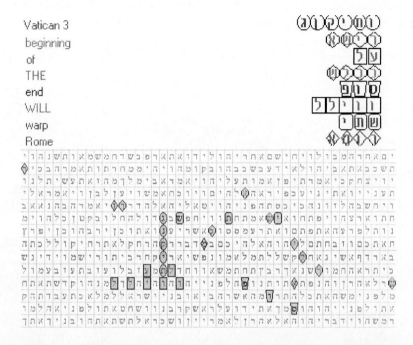

When Vatican III takes place, sweeping changes are headed for the Church. Dogmas will be pitched and blasphemous new tenets will be exchanged for the old. A new morality will be the result of Vatican III, one that provides for abortion, birth control, euthanasia, women priests and whatever "feels good" will be permissible.

In the United States, we are already seeing some of those changes allowed in some dioceses. There is even a push to remove papal authority and for the Church to be headed by a congressional body totally eliminating the pope. No doubt, the alleged documents that are supposedly buried under the Temple Mount will prove, according to the Knights Templar, that Rome is not the center of the Christian world, that a single leader of the Church, the pope, was not what Jesus intended. Even though the Bible clearly states that Jesus founded the

Church upon the rock, St. Peter, we will be dissuaded from believing that gospel. We will then be encouraged to coalesce with the "new" but erroneous dogma, that the rock Jesus was referring to was the Temple Mount and not a person.

The move to have Jerusalem as the world and religious capitol, is gaining ground, clearing the way for the Antichrist to assume the throne in the Third Temple.

Well-placed prelates in Rome believe that the hour of Satan is at hand. With the Church crumbling, these prelates warn, in the book, Shroud of Secrecy, that we must do all that we can before the cock crows for the third time.

Referring to the Church, these prelates state, "It must become, again, the Church of the Crucified Lord and renounce material things and ambition, or risk expulsion from the kingdom of heaven. Indeed, we must all be very careful or we will all lose that treasured kingdom.

There are many priests within the Jesuit order that are working hard at building the New World, a City of Man, and thereby joining the Masons and Communists in the obliteration of the Church and in the end, the world. It goes without saying that not all Jesuits are participating in this vicious behavior. However, there has been a concerted effort on the part of the Father Generals of the order over that past thirty years, to align the Jesuits with Marxist doctrine. While embracing Marxism and in some cases carrying weapons, often times shooting their opponents as in Central America, the Jesuits have clearly run away from Jesus, the namesake of their order.

The Jesuits, who were known for their loyalty to the pope, have all but abandoned the Holy Father. They have made it clear that they will not answer to the pope. If the Jesuits finally get their way by calling for a Vatican III council, Liberation Theology will be at its core. According to Father Malachi Martin, the beginning of the end came with Vatican II when bishops and cardinals interpreted the results as freeing them from "papal totalitarianism."

Some bishops took this to mean that they could interpret doctrine and teach it according to that often skewed perception without having to obey the pope or to consult him.

In the past forty years, modernism has taken over the Church because of a joint effort of Jesuits and Masons. By using, "in the spirit of Vatican II," all kinds of deviations from Church dogma have been excused. Those serious departures have undermined papal authority and dismantled the Church brick by brick.

Yet the Jesuits don't have designs on the Church alone. Rather, they are involved with and are manipulating governments all over the world with their brand of theology meant to advance the New World Order and ultimately supplying us with the Antipope.

In what the Jesuits call the "real church," comprised of men and women who decide for themselves the direction and the concepts of their religion, we see the sickening foundation for a one-world religion, a church universal. The Church Universal promotes social and political causes by trying to wipe out capitalism, no matter what it takes.

The Jesuits and the cadres of socialists who are loosening the shackles of bondage, freeing communities, supposedly to choose their own destinies, destinies based on Marxist principles if some of the Jesuits have their way.

Pope Paul VI tried in vain to stop this modernistic movement and did all he could until he was taken hostage and subsequently killed at the hands of his captors. Each of his successors has done battle with the Marxists. John Paul I was, of course, murdered the night before he was to abolish the Jesuit order. Pope John Paul II has had several attempts on his life because he concurred with John Paul I that the Jesuits had gone too far.

In the end, John Paul II will be murdered, as many prophecies have predicted.

"I saw one of my successors taking flight over the bodies of his brethren. He will take refuge in disguise somewhere; and after a short retirement he will die a cruel death. The present wickedness of the world is only the beginning of the sorrows which must take place before the end of the world."
– St. Pius X – 20th century

"The Pope shall die during these calamities, and the Church will be reduced to the most painful anarchy as a result. Much human blood will be shed in Italy; many cities, towns and castles shall be brought to ruins, causing the death of many thousands of people." –
Capuchin Friar – 18th century

His successor will not be duly elected, but will steal the papacy before the Holy Father dies. This act will illegitimize the papacy and the reign of the Antipope will begin.

Jesus told the apostles that whatever they loosed on earth, would be loosed in heaven and whatever was held bound would also be held bound in heaven. Without the proper transition of power, the Antipope will create new dogmas for the "people of God" to follow and his ultimate cohort, the Antichrist, will eventually enforce those dogmas.

With the May 2001 consistory of Cardinals pushing "themes for our times," it seems the Jesuits have lots of company in their desire to abolish papal primacy. Cardinal Murphy-O'Connor of Westminster, England, seems to be all in favor of doing anything and everything to appease "Universal" Christians and non-Christians, promoting an end to papal authority, citing it as the main obstacle to unity. Indeed, unless one of the "universal" Cardinals sits on St. Peter's throne, a conservative, Roman Catholic pope will delay their plans.

In addition, the dark side has been working overtime in acquiring targets that invariably make the Church look badly, especially in matters of prelates who go too far. One such prelate, Emmanual Milingo, from Zambia, has literally gone off the wall bringing scandal to the Church. Milingo, a former archbishop, recently got married to a 43 year old Korean acupuncturist in a group wedding conducted by Sun Myung Moon.

The exorcist of the Diocese of Rome, Father Gabriele Amorth, said of his long-time friend, Milingo, that he had apparently been brainwashed. It is not that Milingo wasn't already a renegade. In 1983, Milingo was transferred to Rome after charges were leveled against him regarding misusing powers of exorcism and disrupting his diocese. This slap on the wrist did little to curb Milingo's spectacles and exorcisms that he performed without his bishop's permission. He was subsequently asked to resign his post at the Pontifical Council for Migrants and Travelers.

Father Amorth said in a recent interview, that Milingo had been depressed and that the Moonies used this to wear him down. Amorth said the Moonies had in fact kidnapped Milingo. Whatever the case may be, news stories about out-of-control priests are becoming more frequent. Whether priests marry under strange circumstances, or hold nuns captive, molesting them, the press feeds on these events throwing a harsh light on the rest of the Church. All too often, the entire Church is judged for the sins of a few of its clergy.

This is a carefully devised plan that is calling for the end to celibacy and to long held dogmas of the Church. I fully expect outrageous reports to become more prevalent as the era closes. Satanic forces have infiltrated the Vatican for years and it is clear that it is under attack from within as well as from without. The pope has been a target of global forces who would prefer to see him dead. The line has been drawn

THE GATES OF HELL

down the middle of the Church, as the opposing sides square off against one another over assorted social and moral issues as well as the all-important papal primacy.

One of the key backers of the pope is newly elected Cardinal Avery Dulles, who was born on the opposing side of the issue, but had a major change of heart and spirituality that led him to become a prince of the Church. Dulles is the son of John Foster Dulles, a formidable player for the globalists, a member of the Council on Foreign Relations, and participated in the League of Nations. John Foster Dulles was also considered the architect of the post-war era. Avery Dulles' uncle, Allen, was head of CIA and was best known for misleading President Kennedy on the Bay of Pigs operation. His career was dotted with questionable moves and alliances. At best, he was a shadow government leader with un-American ideas. His loyalty, similar to his brother's was to the New World Order.

For the most part, Avery Dulles was brought up in an agnostic Protestant family that had little use for God or for religion.

Through his college days at Harvard University, Avery Dulles studied the writings of Thomas Aquinas, Dante and others. He found himself thinking more about Catholicism and became intrigued with the religion. On Sundays, he noticed that the Sunday Masses in the Cambridge area were always overflowing with people and Sunday evening devotions, which he attended, were also crowded. The future Cardinal asked about becoming a Catholic and was told he needed to talk to a priest, but he had never met any. That hurdle was quickly passed, but the remaining hurdle of informing his parents proved to be a daunting task.

Dulles finally sat down with his parents and told them of his desire to convert to the Catholic faith. They were less than thrilled. His father was actually outright embarrassed by the whole thing and concerned about what his friends in the CFR would think. It got to the point that John Foster Dulles would not speak to his son and eventually cut him completely out of his life.

Avery Dulles was not deterred by this setback. He continued his instructions in the faith and eventually became a Jesuit priest. Cardinal Dulles so far has stuck to the older principles of the Jesuits and has not bought into the Marxist trap of his fellow priests.

Some journalists think Dulles is a CFR plant within the Vatican, or even perhaps a CIA operative. The suggestions that he might be anti-Semitic are also being discussed. There are concerns that he might be like his father and want the total annihilation of the Jews and wants to advance the New World Order platform. Further, the notion that the pope made Dulles a cardinal because the Holy Father buys into the New World Order scheme and the destruction of Israel is unfounded.

I have found nothing that would substantiate that. Instead, Cardinal Dulles appears to be a good man, a humble man, and a man who wants to serve his God, and his Church, and obedient to the pope. It is rather premature to convict the cardinal merely because he was related to men who were members of the CFR.

Dulles' strong arguments against liberalism paint him in a conservative light that would lead his diocese and by his considerable influence, possibly lead the Church away from ruin. He is certainly someone to watch.

Still, there are double agents in the Vatican who not only have a political agenda, but a satanically spiritual program.

I have been asked countless times if the black masses Father Martin wrote about actually transpired in the Church. The answer is yes. They are still being conducted and despicable demonic rituals abound, not only in the Vatican, but also in some churches all over the world.

Yes, there are cardinals within the Vatican who participate in the black masses and truly serve Lucifer. It is becoming more difficult to know which side prelates belong to in this complicated war. We are seeing abuses of all kinds on the part of the clergy. In many cases, parishioners seem to go along with the removal of kneelers, to accept the change of liturgy and to actively take part in bizarre changes in their parishes. Those changes are purposely constructed to make the sacrifice of the Mass null and void.

Currently, the timetable for the end-times may depend on how long the good forces within the Vatican can keep the malevolent forces from taking over the Church entirely. The fight is intense and the evil forces are making inroads, fomenting their position. However, the good forces are delaying their advance. How long they can keep this up is in doubt, but each day they push back the Antichrist's men, the world is given more valuable time to prepare.

One thing is certain, if we are to believe the prophets, Rome is coveted not only by the NWO, but also by Muslim forces. A significant road sign prior to the Warning will be Muslim forces pushing towards Rome and its destruction.

Some people are working the diplomacy angle to open the powerful and reinforced doors to the Vatican. While John Paul II was in Fatima, Gorbachev was meeting with Cardinal Sodano in Rome to discuss the release of the new book, "Martyrdom of Patience," which contains the memoirs of the late Cardinal Casaroli. The Cardinal played an important part in holding Pope Paul VI hostage. This blatant reception for Gorbachev underscores the ties that bind the sinister forces together and attests to the global alliances that have formed to achieve a common goal.

Gorbachev has been a diligent worker and has been spoken of one of the devils incarnate by Our Lady.

*"My child and My children, make it known to
your Senate and your President that the two-
legged demon [Gorbachev], as We address
him, has entered upon your country; and they
are not to be deceived, for he has a major plan
against the United States."*
– Given to Veronica Lueken - June 18, 1990

Our Lady is trying to tell us through various prophets the
danger Gorbachev is to the world. Few people are listening
even though defectors like Stanislav Lunev have told us
hundreds of times about Gorbachev, Putin and the not so
besieged Russia who have the destruction of the United
States as their top priority. We simply fail to notice. If the
media says Russia is on the verge of collapse, that Gorbachev
has retired his "political" aspirations, we simply believe it.
We don't question the news and we fail to make the
connection.

As proof that there are some in the Vatican working with
and for the communists, Cardinal Angelo Sodano, Secretary
of State at the Vatican, has reiterated that the Vatican-
Moscow Treaty is still in effect. Cardinal Casaroli, Sodano's
predecessor, backed that treaty which appeases Russia.
Heaven was very concerned about that treaty. Our Lady
warned that this conciliation could have terrible results,
eventually bringing about the deaths of millions and the
enslavement of millions more. Sodano is also in favor of this
soft line toward communism, and Gorbachev was delighted
with this new tact.

By meeting with Sodano to launch Casaroli's memoirs,
Gorbachev virtually spit in the eye of John Paul II, a man
with whom he claims to have a newfound friendship.
Gorbachev was aware and involved in the Bulgarian plot to
assassinate the Holy Father and obviously felt that his unholy
alliances with evil forces within the Vatican could now be
revealed.

Russia is not only an enemy of Rome, but also the nemesis of the United States and all freedom loving people. Stanislav Lunev warned Congress about Russia's intent to take over the United States. He sees a pre-emptive nuclear strike on this country as imminent.

In 1962, Pope John XXIII arranged clandestine negotiations with the Kremlin. He sent Cardinal Tisserant to represent the Vatican in the talks designed to allow Russian Orthodox clergy to attend the now infamous Vatican II.

The Kremlin said it would agree, but the Vatican had to promise something in return. The promise to which Cardinal Tisserant agreed involved the silence on the part of the Vatican towards Russia and its communistic regime. Through Cardinal Tisserant, the Vatican agreed that it would not attack the Russian communists in Vatican II. The Vatican-Moscow Treaty is still in force today.

Many cardinals signed this treaty much to heavens consternation. The essence and the very existence of that treaty has kept true peace at bay. Unless Pope John Paul II rescinds the treaty, there will be no lasting peace with Russia. Until the Pope consecrates Russia to Our Lady, we are headed for annihilation.

On the surface, the treaty would help lessen the persecution of Catholics in communist countries. However, thousands of Catholics, including the clergy, were still tortured and killed, adequate reason to nullify the agreement.

Our Lady's peace plan, initiated at Fatima, was abandoned. The Vatican may just have sold its soul to the murderers of the "communist regime" as Sodano prefers to call Russia.

Sodano has done despicable things against the Holy Father and took great delight in 1998, when he lauded the works of Hans Kung to the world press. Kung happens to despise John Paul II, calling him a "despot." He is also a heretic who has denied all Catholic dogma.

In 1980 Kung was ordered by John Paul II to be stripped of his theological credentials. By Sodano publicly cheering Kung, he made a statement that he, too, is against the Holy Father. It surprised no one when Sodano foisted the pseudo Third Secret of Fatima upon the world. It was the last block to the platform of the Antichrist. It has been under construction for nearly forty years within the Vatican, and the unveiling of the super global "team" is just about here.

Sodano isn't just busy within the Vatican. He has been hard at work as a pivotal ramrod for the International Criminal Court and is pushing the global UN agenda. His construct of "crimes yet to be defined," will someday imprison right to life advocates, and eventually, those of us who fail to follow the Antichrist.

Advocating that Catholic priests could be arrested and brought before the ICC to divulge confessions of "known criminals," Sodano is a true gem in the championship belt of the New World Order.

Obviously, if Sodano released the real Third Secret of Fatima, the UN's future plans for the world would be revealed. He has a vested interest in lying to the world.

Sources indicate it was Sodano and Sodano only, who wished to release the false Third Secret. By his announcement at Fatima on May 13, 2000, the Holy Father was "trapped" into agreeing with him in public. Then Sodano drafted his deceitful documents and shoved them down our throats.

Sodano, talking out of both sides of his mouth, said that the Third Secret contained prophecy from scripture, although those events were already passed, an outright lie.

It is amazing that an entire committee of theologians had to draft a commentary so that the world could understand what a ten-year-old girl in Fatima already knew from the plain words of the Blessed Mother.

We don't need any more proof that the Vatican has truly fallen to Satan.

The world lost a major battle to evil and now we are in for the fight of our lives.

The clergy is not alone in their globalist philosophies that are poisoning the world. There are movements working under the guise of religious entities that claim to be formed under principles of the Gospel. In reality, they promote the same agenda as Gorbachev and Sodano.

The Focolare Movement is just such a group with a penchant for global issues. Once again, we see people doing things for "good causes," appearing cosmetically clear and fresh, but needing major reconstructive surgery once the make-up is scrubbed away.

Blossoming in the midst of World War II, the Focolare Movement was started by Chiara Lubich and her friends. They embrace the spirituality of unity like a long lost love. They tout a life of "authenticity," but in the end, the veneer wears thin.

The group is trying to push the Catholic world into full communion with other denominations and to push for openness to all faiths and beliefs.

There are 18 different branches of the movement, setting goals for families, children, priests, men or women. "Little towns" of Focolare members have appeared and have become involved with businesses. Currently, there are four million members.

Recently, 85 cardinals took part in one of Focolare's global meetings, backing the movement's socialist agenda. Apparently, the group is concerned with giving globalization a "face" for people to see as a positive front for the burning of boundaries. Their acceptance of other cultures will only last until a particular culture disagrees with their Marxist hearts. The Focolare Movement appears in the Bible Code and the results are on the next page.

Found In Genesis 31:43

FOCOLARE
eighteen
branch
plotting
destruction
OF
THE
faith
from
within

As the rats flee the sinking city of Rome, headed for Jerusalem, and the Reign of the Antichrist, their disease permeates the air and infects the majority of the world. This particular plague will be one of the most devastating of the end times.

Conclusion

Perhaps the most remarkable finding in the code and also the most significant one is the Third Secret. It is the one code upon which all others rest.

The evidence is clear that Rome released a fake, trying to quell our fears about the future. We must prepare ourselves for the overwhelming reality that will soon strike terror in our hearts. Catastrophic times are promised without the dedication of Russia to the Immaculate Heart.

Without this dedication, the rest of the NOW plans will come to frightful fruition. Billions of people are scheduled to die and hearts will fail when thrust into the sordid reality of our future.

The Bible Code gives us proof that the enemy is real and formidable. It also gives us magnificent proof that God is real and stronger than the dark side. He is talking to us, showing us what is just up the road. God is telling us, out of His abundant love, that we're in mortal danger. The enemy has been identified.

If we don't do something to stop this semi that is barreling down on all of us, we'll hit the windshield of this monster truck like a frail bug. With God's help, we can set up a detour for the end-times, if we would only pray. We can't turn a blind eye to the bright lights of the NOW vehicle, nor should we be blinded like a deer caught in the high beams. We can, however, change the grade of the road, making the drive difficult for the other side and thereby slowing their momentum.

This book is merely a sampling of what is in store. There are other means scheduled to be utilized by the Antichrist. There are also codes in the Bible identifying them for what they are. I encourage you to do your homework, get the facts and then do something about it. Prayer is the ultimate weapon, the consummate weigh station through which peace can be obtained.

> *"And I say unto thee: Thou art Peter, and*
> *upon this rock I will build my church, and*
> *the gates of hell shall not prevail against it."*
> *Matt. 16:18*

Index

D

Daniel · 12
DARPA · 24, 26
Defense Advanced Research Projects Agency · 24
Department of Justice · 94
Diarrheic shellfish poisoning · 81
DNA · 27
DOJ · 94
Dome of the Rock · 125, 129, 130, 131, 132
Douay-Rheims · 11
DSP · 81
Dugway · 32
Dulles · 174, 175

E

Ebola · 44, 45, 46, 47, 66
Elijah Solomon · 9
England · 55, 113, 172
EPA · 63, 73, 90
EU · 57, 58, 95, 96
Europe · 36, 48, 51, 52, 61, 66, 71, 75, 85, 95, 117, 137, 138, 139
European Union · 55, 57, 95

F

FAA · 24
FAO · 57
Father Malachi Martin · 142, 145, 171

G

H

O

P

About The Author

Kathleen Keating is an investigative journalist and author of the international bestseller, The Final Warning: Your Survival Guide to The New Millennium. She publishes a monthly newsletter, The Messenger, bringing the world the latest end-time breaking reports.

Kathleen writes an immensely popular weekly Internet column, The Keating Perspective, and is currently working on two end-time novels.

Kathleen's website
www.kathleenkeating.com

The Messenger
www.materdeipress.com

Want more information on this subject?
You may be interested in some of these titles.

The Final Warning, by Kathleen Keating. The international best selling book that rocked the world. An in-depth look at politics, prophecy and the people behind it all.

The Messenger, Kathleen's monthly newsletter. Kathleen and her team of experts bring you the best of prophecy, current events, Bible Codes, and much more every month.

The Enigma Files. Spend two hours with Kathleen and her guests as they strive to unlock conspiracies and bring you the truth.

Check the order form in the back of the book for more information!

Coming Soon…

Noise of the Mourning: The political thriller that started it all.

Silence of the Evening: The knockout sequel to Noise of the Mourning, guaranteed to send chills up your spine.

Torn Sky: A novel based on the research behind the international best seller, The Final Warning.

Brother Love: Think the Antichrist won't deceive the elect? This novel will change that view forever.